MICHAEL AN ENDTIME SIGN

By:

CAROLYN SMITH PHILLIPS

"Michael An Endtime Sign," by Carolyn Smith Phillips. ISBN 978-1-60264-560-8.

Manufactured in the United States of America.

MICHAEL AN

ENDTIME SIGN

BY: CAROLYN SMITH PHILLIPS

Isaiah 60: "AWAKE, ARISE, SHINE; for your light is come,

And

The Glory of the LORD <u>is (risen)</u>

<u>Rose</u> upon you."

My Prayer "is to be one as God is one. LORD, Let my spirit, soul and body be one in you, awakened, risen and shining on this earth as it is in heaven"!

ACKNOWLEDGMENTS

I want to thank The Most High God, Father, Mother, Son, and yet One Creator of all things, The Archangel Gabriel and all the spiritual saints and angels, also, Rev. Sylvia & Rev. Early Thomas. It is with deep gratitude and appreciation for all you have done for me. My Husband Sam and Children: Tammy, Jay and Penny, Stepchildren: Wendy and Nell. My grandchildren Michael, Michelle, Alexis, Joseph {Jo Jo}, Jayden and Jayson, my step-grandchildren; Lil Robert, Austin, Wyatt and Kalee and my god-grandson Cedric. Special thanks for my daughter Tammy and her best friends Jennifer and Wendy who keep my computer going.

I also want to acknowledge my doctors who have helped me these past ten years to get some of my quality life back. Making it possible for me to write again. Dr. Richard Goulah, Robin Harmer, P.A., and all their nurses and staff, of South Boston VA. Dr. Jesse Stem, and Kamal Chantal P.A., Dr. Murray Joiner and all of their staff of Lynchburg Va.. It is because of all of you and your kindness that I am able physically to write again. Thank you. May you see me completely healed. Please know that you are appreciated for the effects you make to keep me pain free as much as possible.

The Gazette-Virginian, especially Cathy, The News and Record of South Boston VA, The Southside Messenger, The South Hill Enterprise of South Hill, Va., The Lynchburg News and Advance & The Burg of Lynchburg Va. The Piedmont Shopper & Danville Bee of Danville Va. And The Courier-Times, of Roxboro, N. C. thank you.

Also I would like to thank my instructor at The Institute of Children's Literature of West Redding, CT. for helping me to continue my studies in writing and graduate. Thank you.

My Publisher, Editor, Designer, and Staff for their commitment, ideals and work in getting this book to print in such a beautiful way. Thank you.

My readers thank you. May God bless each and every one of you according to His will and keep you well and safe. Be blessed.

About the Author

Carolyn Smith Phillips of Halifax Virginia, is a wife, mother of three children and stepmother of two. A grandmother of six grandchildren and a step-grandmother of four and a God-grandmother of one. She is also a Toy-Chinese Chihuahua Breeder and a published author.

Before her disability and retirement she was a real estate investor and paralegal. She also was a counselor who worked with unmarried pregnant teens and abused children for the Southern Baptist Association of Jacksonville, Fl. There she had her own radio talk show for six years and a regular guest on several Christian Television shows. She now resides in her hometown.

The author attended Halifax County schools where she graduated and continued her education at Keysville Community College, Keysville Va., Danville Community College, Danville Va., and, Old Dominion of Virginia, in Norfolk, Va. Her subjects were real estate one and two, real estate law, real estate finance, real estate appraisal, physiology and sociology. As well as the Century Twenty-One School of Real Estate. She also attended W.V. Grant Ministries where she received a minister's certificate, and The First Superet Light Branch Church of Washington, D.C. where she finished twelve lesson course in Spiritual Light and received her instructor's certificate. The author continued her love and studies with the Institute of Children's Literature of West Ridding, CT.

Contents

Introduction

Michael, An Endtime Sign is about a twenty-two year old girl who was told she was sterile. But after three dreams by the same Archangel that announced Jesus and other babies in the Bible appeared to her mother, this twenty two year old girl conceived. She gave birth to a baby in spite of a nightmare experience in the hospital. After a near death experience and her belief in God she brought forth a baby boy. You will read about the first dream and what that dream said about her conception. The second dream and what the Archangel announced about the type of delivery she would have. Then the third dream about his move to Halifax Virginia and the age of this baby.

You will read about preachers and prophets who announced he was full of the Holy Spirit at birth. Announced he was a child of light and an endtime sign of new beginning and new age. Some of you will learn a new way of studying the Bible and a new way of believing in God's words and promises.

You will read about the fears and doubts, battles and background of a family with so many hardships. The struggle of two families coming together with loads of pain for the losses they already suffered.

CHAPTER ONE

THE IMPOSSIBLE BIRTH...OR WAS IT?

CHAPTER ONE

THE IMPOSSIBLE BIRTH...OR WAS IT?

It was a hot spring afternoon, May 13th, 1988, in Jacksonville, Florida, when Tammy, my oldest daughter, came bursting through the front door screaming and crying, "I'm sterile, Mama, I'm sterile. The doctor said all the tests came back. I can never have a baby." Shaking the papers at me with such anguish and fear, she continued, "This is the fifth test they've done, and the specialists say all the tests show the same thing. I am sterile."

Right away I knew this doctor had destroyed all her faith in a miracle. Tammy had known since she was thirteen that she may be sterile, which was caused by a drug given to me when I was six months pregnant to prevent a miscarriage with her. I knew immediately that I had to destroy those negative seeds that had been planted in her by that doctor. I looked up from my Bible reading and said as sternly and compassionately as I could, "Who are you going to believe, Tammy, God or man? God opened a ninety-year-old woman's womb {Sara} and gave her a son in the Bible. He can certainly open a twenty-two year old womb and do the same for you. The Bible is an example of what we are to believe and live by. Either we believe it or we don't. We have believed together since you were thirteen that God would heal this problem if there was one and give you a baby in his timing. Now believe it!"

Tammy looked up at me with the cruelest set of eyes I had ever seen and just stared. I stared back as I waited for her to decide whom she would believe, God or man. She walked past me with no answer and went to her room, slamming the door behind her.

I knew she had battled with faith after her daddy decided to take a different route in life and divorced us. After the divorce she doubted her own self and her own worthiness as well. I felt those were the reasons she had postponed college, 'take a leave,' is what she said. She was a straight A student all the way through school. Loved books and writing since she was two years old. Had scholarships to colleges most kids dreamed about. But I also knew we had raised her to believe the Bible was God's promise to us. That God was a God of his word and kept his promises, not like humans. She had been taught that what God had did for one person in that Bible, he would do for us all. I had to believe the Bible was just that simple and had taught her it was.

I felt this was one test where God just had to prove himself or she would turn to the world and disbelief. She had already started testing the worldly waters, so to speak. Did she really believe what she had been taught? Or did she just say she believed out of fear? Did she have that deep-seated faith that had carried her through school and other situations? Only time would tell us.

Tammy had been raised in an Independent Baptist church and went to Christian school. She had also lived with a mama who had had dreams, visions and had seen angels since she was six years old. She had witnessed her mother's faith shaken after the divorce. That deep faith in God's word was rooted and grounded in her, that I choose to believe. No divorce could take that from her or me, I told myself. That was what I was holding on to.

One of the hardest lessons even for adults is that God made us each an individual and God does not interfere when we decide to go a different route. I had taught all my children that God is still God. Our job was to trust him. I had taught that God knew what was best. Those trials were the only opportunities for our soul development and growth. The word of God was the only place I saw truth. It had to be truth!

At this point in time, though, Tammy didn't believe our life was at the best level. She wanted her family together like it used to be. She wanted both parents. Yet both parents had already re-married and she had an extended family. Her three-

year prayer to God to put her parents back together hadn't been answered. Her doubts about God had risen to haunt her mind.

I silently prayed, "Lord, you know what is best. I know your word says ask and believe and you will receive. You know we prayed for their daddy to come home to us and he didn't. You know the kids don't believe you hear our prayers anymore. I'm trying to understand your will, even when I don't. To them the divorce is proof you don't hear us. But I know you do hear us. Your word says so. Lord, I need you to prove to them that you keep your word and hear all our prayers. Lord, I need you to show us that you control all things, in control and out of control, even when it's painful. Lord you know, Wendy and Nell, Sam's girls, believe you are a mean God for letting their mama die with cancer. I need some help here. I fear we will lose them to the world and we don't want that, Lord. This is one prayer we all have prayed as a family, to be answered with a baby. One if answered could build the bridge Sam and I have longed to connect us together as one family. Open Tammy's womb and give her a baby like you did Sarah in the Bible, and like you did Elizabeth and Mary. Prove you are greater than any drug. Prove you are love. Prove you care about us, Lord. Now I thank you, Father God, in Jesus. For I believe you heard me. I choose to believe you have sent the answer. I believe you will strengthen us and give us peace. We will await your manifestation. Amen."

Within seconds I found myself praying again. Knowing it was my own fear. Repenting and confessing my own fears I felt within. Shaken faith from past prayers not answered the way I wanted them. I repented for justifying myself for being blunt with Tammy. I repented for the feelings of guilt. For not hugging and comforting her with loving words. My own doubts arose from within me. "Lord, you spoke those words through me to Tammy, didn't you? Please tell me you did. Help her to receive them? Help us to understand what your will is. Forgive us for being so confused about your will. Enlighten us in your words so we can worship and obey you. Remove our confusion. We need you. We need your peace within. We need to know what your plan and purpose for us is. Remove our doubts."

Again I prayed. "Lord, the prayers not answered my way are spinning in my head. My own battles within need to go, Lord. Help me Lord! Give us some hope. Give us assurance that you listen, that you care. Forgive us for every time we disobeyed you. Help us to do better. We feel we don't deserve your presence or gifts. But that is why Jesus died for us. Isn't it? We are not to work for it now, right? Didn't Jesus die to make us worthy of your gifts and presence? Your word says you listen always. Help me to believe. Are you listening always? Why so silent, Lord? Speak to us. Talk to us. Tell us something, Lord. We need a little hope to keep on. Forgive me for all my sins. Wash me clean. Forgive me for the sins I will do before the day is finished. I choose to believe you hear us. Thank you Lord."

Silence filled the whole house. Was that my answer? Five teenagers and two young adults, and yet all I felt was a still silence. Was God in the silence? What does silence mean? What kind of an answer is silence?

Soon I realized that 4 p.m. had turned into 5 p.m. and time to start dinner. Sam would be home by 6:00, ready to eat. I surely didn't need to set him off. I didn't want to hear his loud mouth today. I slowly got up from my recliner and dragged myself to the kitchen as I called to the children to come and help. Instead of help I received more silence. Not a sound came from any of the five bedrooms. Silence was a great gift with five teens most of the time, but not today. I opened cabinets to see what to prepare. Then I slammed them shut, thinking they would come help if they heard it. I yelled, "Staying away from mean mama, I see?" I shouted down the hall again, "Give me a break here. Come help with dinner." But the silence was like a thick smoke that filled that big house. I pulled out pots and pans and tried to make enough noise that they would come out to see. But that didn't happen. Music always calmed my nerves so I turned on the radio, but not one door opened. I moved around the kitchen, singing as loud as I could, but with no luck.

Sammy came in and wanted to know why the kids weren't in the kitchen helping. He was always straightforward and to the point. I updated him on Tammy. They were mad with me or used it as an excuse not to help, I ended the conversation with.

"Hell!" Sam said. "That's no excuse not to be in this kitchen. We have to eat." He started yelling down the hall, "Get in here. Get in here now and help your mama fix supper. Get that table set and let's eat."

I heard doors open then. I heard swift feet running up the hall. Once in the kitchen, they were still mad as hornets at me. But they moved quickly to get the table set and the tea poured. They knew their daddy wasn't going to hear their complaints or thoughts regardless, of what it was. Sam's loud and authoritative voice came in handy many times with one son, a son-in-law, and four daughters. Five children in the house meant a lot of noise, fussing, laughter, and games. Someone was mad all the time and someone was fussing. Sam and I prayed for silence many times, but this silence wasn't the same.

At the table Sam spoke grace and ended it as usual with, dig in. Sam already had his arms stretched across the table to block Jay from the chicken. A little game they played to see who could eat the most. The girls would yell, have some manners, daddy. Sam yelled back at them, bananas! Where are the bananas?

You embarrass us they would shout back. Their daddy was regular filling his plate, enough for two people, while they fussed. Then they would yell back, we can't take you anywhere, daddy. You act like a pig. Oh, that would make Sam's night. Then he would dig in like a hungry pig, made sounds like a pig, and lick his lips with his big tongue stuck out, all up in their faces he leaned across the table, laughing at them and them calling him crazy and other silly names. Jay dug in the cream potatoes right behind him. By the time all the plates were served I would get up and remove the empty bowls from the middle of the table, making room for eye contact. Then say, "That's enough. Let's have some respect." This ended the playing.

While eating, we discussed any family business or event on anyone's mind. Unless someone was in trouble, then time was set apart for private discussions. Mealtime was the only time we all sat as a family to discuss anything else, though. Such busy lives we all lived, but it made the time pass fast.

Tammy, age twenty-two, married to Tony, had her home but stayed at our house most of the time. She drove a school bus until she decided if she was going back to college or what. She also ate at our house more than hers.

Jay, sixteen, had school, girls, and football, just to name a few. Being the star player on his team opened the door for many invitations and dates. He was always on the run.

Wendy, fifteen, was a straight A student with high honors, church friends, and church work. Plus she had her own chores around the house like dishes, clothes, and cleaning her room, along with many others.

Nell, age eleven, was a student who had to work hard for good grades, but had a lot of common sense when it came to working with her hands or money. A daddy's girl who hung out helping him at the television repair shop. Sometimes at the flea market on weekends if she wasn't with her friends.

Penny, age ten, the youngest, was a mama's girl and a smart student that hated homework. We called her lazy in a joking way. Anything that pertained to physical labor she complained or had a headache, but she did it.

With Sam and I being in the real estate investment business, we always had physical labor to do. Rentals needed repairs when tenants moved out. Fixer-uppers we purchased needed work for resale. Plus he had the television repair shop and flea market hobby. I had the radio and television talk shows that Penny attended with me. There was Aunt Sylvia and Uncle Early, whom we loved dearly and made time for everyday along with church and chores. There were no free rides.

Penny was also the good Samaritan, she loved giving to people. If she heard of a need in the neighborhood she would meet it one way or another, usually with our stuff. If a student was bullied, she was there to protect them. I remember once I came home and she had given our dinner away. I had cooked the night before because we had a tight line that night to get chores done and church. She said the mama was sick and the daddy broke his leg and the kids needed to eat. That was Penny. When asked what we would eat, she answered we were all to fat anyway. We could miss one night.

At home Penny was used to Tammy or me doing for her. But rules had changed since Wendy and Nell came into the family. Penny didn't like change. Usually she and Nell were the topic of discussion because they both complained rather than do their chores. So yes, Jay and Wendy did have more free time because they did their work and earned it. We had house rules posted on the hall wall and it was important everyone obeyed them because of our schedules. One of the rules was, if you eat you must work. If you want money for dates and movies, you had to earn it. To run a household as large as ours we had to be organized. Organization and order was very important. Everyone had to do their part and work as a team without fuss. Each child had a daily planner and we discussed at mealtime what was accomplished and what wasn't. What was accomplished each day determined how they spent their free time and what privileges they had.

But this night everyone was silent. The daily planner wasn't on their minds, Tammy was. Sam jumped in with, "Don't everyone jump in at once now." Then Jay broke loose with his list of wants. That opened the floor for Wendy, Nell and Penny telling him he was selfish. He never thought about anything but himself. Jay looked as if what? What do you mean? Jay lived in his own little world. He got blamed for getting more rights and wants because he was the only boy. Jay could smile that one away and say, 'You're right.' He had a good heart and a sense of humor that could make a dog laugh. But his wants was his main focus. Unless it pertained to him, he didn't bother. He and Sam had a motto, which they lived by: "When you live with five girls in the same house, someone is always mad. Get used to it and go on."

Not one word about Tammy's tests was spoken. When she jumped up suddenly and ran back to her room, everyone knew she couldn't handle the usual dinner conversation. Fussing back and forth at each other to see who would win the battle and get their way with mom and dad. Silence filled the room except for Jay. He wanted to know what her problem was. But before anyone could answer him, Tammy was going through the sliding glass doors. "Going over to Tony's grandmother's to get Tony. Will stay awhile so don't wait up," she said, closing the door. That usually meant she would go to her house.

Wendy filled Jay in on Tammy's problem as everyone got up, cleared the table and washed dishes. Jay's expression changed and we all could see that bothered him. Tammy not having a baby touched all our hearts. We all knew we couldn't help her. It was God or no one. We all had been taught how wonderful and loving God was, and yet we all had suffered deep loss and pain. We wondered where this loving God was for us at times. But Jay in his own way just looked up and asked, "Well, Mama, didn't you pray?" I answered with a nod.

He replied, "Well then, everything will be all right. What about the football game Friday night? Are we going or what?"

Several days passed and not one word about the tests was spoken, and none about my reply. One by one they would come and whisper to me, "Is Tammy okay?"

I would answer each time, "Yes. Don't mention the tests to anyone. If anyone asked, you just say God is working it out." They all agreed.

We waited from day to day to see if God would give us a baby or would it be another disappointment. Tammy didn't mention it and acted like she was all right with it. Whatever would be her answer, but we could see she was hiding her pain. Around Tony she did smile and laugh like it didn't matter. We all knew he was good for her. He could get her spirits up when no one else could. He had such a carefree way about him that he could get us all laughing.

Each of us had our own lists of disappointments. We pretended we had surrendered them to God at church, but inside we knew we still felt that pain. We wanted God to work them out the way we wanted. We didn't really know anything about God's will. Uncle Early and Aunt Sylvia had been teaching us, but we were babes at it. All of us pouted, complained, got angry and made excuses. We all battled with our feelings every day and kept right on being angry and hating everything that we didn't like or want.

What did the kids want? They wanted God to make things like they were before Geraldine died with cancer and Bernard left. We all knew that wasn't going to happen. We did the best we could to get along even with the battles that we all continued to battle with inside, the battle with our own emotions with anger and hate each day. We put up a good front around most people, especially church people.

A preacher and counselor told us all that we were our worst enemies. And until we overcame anger, disappointment and hate, we would stay in the war zone within ourselves and with each other. We knew he was right. We just didn't know how to win the war. Our friends listened but had little advice in helping us to overcome. Most Christians told us to trust Jesus. Well sorry, that wasn't enough. Studying the words of Jesus did give us peace within. Going over to Aunt Sylvia's and Uncle Early's and them speaking the word over us helped more than anything else, in my opinion. But as soon as we faced the littlest problem we blew up as usual.

This baby was our only hope of this family having a chance to survive. There just was too much old negative baggage, as one counselor put it. If we were going to have a real caring, loving family, it had better happen soon. It was the rope we could hang on to until we all healed within. It was the thread that could bind us together as one family. If this baby didn't come forth, Sam and I both knew our marriage was over. The children were just too unhappy the way it was. A baby. If God gave us a baby, he had his work cut out for him. Would he know what kind of a messed up family he would be born in?

Some religions believe that we are a spirit and we choose our earthly family and the situations each of us will work out for our soul development. Another religion believes that we come into these flesh bodies and are totally in the dark as to who we are and who created us. Would this baby know he would be the love of our life? Could he be the salvation of our marriage? Would he even know that our marriage was riding on his shoulders? Would he know that he was the hope that might bind a dysfunctional family together?

This baby was the first goal we all shared together since we had married and became a family. It was the first time the whole family stood together, praying and hoping that God would give Tammy and Tony a baby. Uncle Early and Aunt

Sylvia and every close friend that didn't think we were crazy stood with us. This family had come together, believed together, prayed together and asked God to fix Tammy. We knew only God could. This was 'our baby', we called it.

Then there's Tony, the baby's daddy, the love of Tammy's life. Everyone loved him, his humor, and the way he just popped up and made himself part of the family. He was fun and full of life, always joking about something. The way he acted around Tammy told everyone that he loved her dearly. His blond hair and blue eyes and slim figure made him very attractive. Tammy was jealous of him, and Sam and Jay played on that. But Tony had a way with people. It was hard to tell him no. No matter what it was he could talk Tammy into it, most of the time he would talk the rest of us into it too. We laughed about it and yet let him do anyway. He just had that zest about him.

He had a little drinking problem and that concerned me, but he must have loved being around us because every day after work he would be at our house to help. He would work all afternoon for Sam for nothing but a carton of beer. With rental houses, there was always work to be done. If anyone could get Tammy in a good mood and keep her in it while we waited on God's answer, it would be Tony.

Tony was such a good-hearted person also. He never wanted to make waves, he called it. Being very close to his grandparents, if they weren't at our house they were there. Even though Tammy and Tony had their own home up the street from us, they stayed around his family or hers most of the time. Sam kept telling them they could save money if they just moved in with us and paid us rent. But Tony liked his own place to crash, he would say. Sam and Jay figured another man in the house to shoot pool with, throw horseshoes, and help with rentals and yard work would be great. Tony would give the men a little leverage, they would say, with so many girls in the house. Tammy being with Tony was the best place she could be.

Tony had been a refreshing addition. His laughter and jokes made us forget about the sadness in our lives. Always going around hugging whoever was fussing and get them in a good mood. Somehow he just kept everyone in a good mood when he was around. We loved him and Tammy being there and never wanted them to go or do anything without us. If this baby was anything like his daddy's personality, we knew he would be the love and joy all bundled up in one little body for all of us. We were already dreaming about this baby in our minds as we discussed what it would be like for Tammy and Tony to have a baby.

We had moved to Jacksonville to start over with our extended family in the hopes of changing our house of pain into a loving, caring family. Sam's kids had a step-mama they didn't want. They had no answers as to why God would let their sweet mama die. My kids had a step-daddy they didn't want. They wanted answers as to how a loving God could just allow their daddy to walk out and leave us. Sam and I certainly didn't have any answers. We were just trying to build a new relationship with what we had. We knew we had five children in need of a home. We knew all of us needed a heart and emotional healing. Tony being the new addition helped us to accomplish that a little. So a baby would too, we thought. Along with Aunt Sylvia and Uncle Early, a new baby just might be the answer for all of us and change our separated family into one family unit.

The kids were always coming up with something to start an argument, always Wendy, Nell and Sam against me, Tammy, Jay and Penny. Sam and I were caught in the middle every time. Tony was the go-between many times because he could see all points of view and laughed at all of us, making us feel so silly for even being mad.

Have you ever lived in a house with five rebellious teens? It was no picnic for any of us. But we felt God sent us Uncle Early, Aunt Sylvia, and Tony to help us. We didn't know how Tony felt about the doctor's news. We knew he wanted a little boy. Tammy didn't talk much about hers and Tony's relationship, and we didn't ask too many questions. She said he was disappointed and had gone to his grandmother's after work, and she had come by to tell us the news. Being with him and his family at this time was a good thing. That day played over and over in our heads and a part of our conversations for days.

After Tammy left that night, the night of the doctor's disappointing news, I had called and told Aunt Sylvia and Uncle Early what the doctor said. Also what had flew out of my mouth about God and Sarah. They were in agreement with us. Don't repeat what the doctors said to anyone else, they said. They told me to hold on to my faith and know that God hears every request. Aunt Sylvia and Uncle Early were the strongest people we knew in faith at that time. They were the reason we had decided to choose Jacksonville to start over. So for every day after that night we held strong to our faith in God answering our prayer for a baby.

We had stayed in their home for two weeks prior to moving to Jacksonville and witnessed them stand on God's word every day. Like a daily habit, their every movement and word was God's word. I had longed to be taught by such faithful people. Sam and I both had such a hunger for the truth. We both had been taught so much religion and hurt deeply by it and the people in it. But Aunt Sylvia and Uncle Early lived daily what they preached, and it was refreshing. They had already set the groundwork for this test of faith. All we had to do was obey.

Aunt Sylvia and Uncle Early told us we were supposed to bring heaven to earth. We were sent to earth for that purpose, chosen by God as a child to live in God's presence daily. To manifest his glory in us and upon this earth, that he loved us just the way we were. That if we had anything displeasing to God then he would use the Holy Spirit to clean us up, that God wanted us happy, healthy and wealthy. WOW! That sure was different from what we had been taught.

They taught that our job was to live the best we could in the flesh bodies. To study the word and apply one spiritual law at a time until we overcame one bad habit or disobedient act, and let God do the rest. That every time we opened the New Testament, God would enlighten us. That was His way of talking to us, through the written word until he could talk to us and we hear him in that still voice within us or audibly. Practicing good habits every day was the key to pleasing our heavenly Father, they said. Bring God forth out of our temples (bodies) on this earth in such a way he couldn't be denied, they said. Christ's words would give us hope, strength and wisdom.

The Holy Spirit was the action side of God that got things done. He living within would do the obeying and the work. Focus on Christ, they said, and grow up into the God level. Humble yourself and surrender to the living word. Learn which voice was God's and which one was flesh. When in doubt, go to the word and see what Jesus did.

They made us feel special with God. The apple of God's eye, they told us we were. Wow! No one had ever told us that. Then Uncle Early would add with a smile, "If you can't find it in that written word, then God is going to do a new thing in you and with you." So either way we were to believe in what we wanted and believe that God would give it.

Uncle Early said pain was the reason God had so 'few'. Then he gave us scripture for that word, 'few' manifesting God today. Being a Christian is painful, he would say. Purification means God washes all the darkness out daily. That is painful to the flesh because the flesh loved darkness, our mind and emotional battles were our own flesh fighting against God. The Holy Spirit's work was to dig around our roots, to let light in. He said we were like trees. God rooted around our roots, pruned our branches and helped us to grow up. Every tree needed to produce fruit after its own kind. Then Uncle Early would smile again and scratch his head and say, "For someone else to come along and see our delicious fruit. Pluck it off of us and eat it." Then he would add, have you ever seen an apple tree eat its own fruit? Pain comes because humans don't like change. That was our battle!

Aunt Sylvia and Uncle Early had such a way of explaining what God sent Jesus in us to do that even a child could understand. Just to name a few of their golden nuggets that they shared with us, I hope will build up your faith. I hope will give you a little more understanding as to what God has been doing for the past two thousand years. How he has been getting us ready for this day, for this generation. When you ask God to use you, he will clean you up, they taught. When he enters your temple with that entire garbage, he will throw that entire garbage out before he moves in to dwell. The moment you invite him in and surrender your temple to him, he begins. Pain is a good thing. It means you were attached to some garbage. God will wrestle with you until he has won. He will turn your table over. He will sweep and mop your floors. He will dust every crack and corner. He will throw out everything that is not clean and pure. All you have to do is surrender daily. You will feel the freedom and the cleanness of every cleaned space. God likes organization. Do you really want God to move into your dirty house and sleep and eat? Jesus went to the Father when he finished his work. He sent the Holy Spirit to clean us up. He guides us and teaches us how to keep our temples clean once it is clean. He will make us whiter than snow. He will fill us up with all goodness. The flesh doesn't like that. That old ego is full of pride, they would say. That ego will fight for every inch of space within you. But have no fear. Greater is God within you than that old ego. When you get tired of fighting, you will surrender to the Holy Spirit. "Can you handle it?" Uncle Early would ask. "Do you have the courage to endure the pain? Do you have the courage to surrender and just let God have his way?"

Only a few are truly willing to suffer for God, he would say. Only a few are willing to scream, holler and endure such pain. It takes courage to serve God. No room for cowards in God's family. The cowards will try to tease with lust, drugs and all sorts of worldly stuff. Do you know why? Because they are too chicken to suffer and want you to be a chicken, too. Only eagles will survive. Only a few will say, keep it up God. Keep it up until you own all the space within me. Here I am. I give myself to you. Do whatever you like with me.

Uncle Early said we would stay on earth until we have developed into the level of consciousness we came to earth to do. Some will never see physical death. He believed he was one of those. He continued to teach us day by day. It required us to own and manifest light in these bodies. Then we wouldn't see physical death. That God was waiting on us. He said all that religion would have to be washed out of us and we would be made new with new thoughts, new emotions, new desires and dreams. That we are to throw out the negative and replace it with God thoughts. Meditate on God thoughts. We were to think about it every second until it became a part of us, oneness, he said. That was our purpose for coming to Jacksonville. Don't jump out of the car going a hundred miles per hour on interstate 95 or you may get killed, he would say. They made us feel proud to suffer. Proud that God chose to take Geraldine to heaven and leave Wendy and Nell for Sam and I to raise. Proud that Bernard left me and moved on to his new beginnings so we could move on up in God, as he put it. He made pain a gift. Consider yourself blessed to suffer for what is right, he would say. Did they know they were preparing us for Tammy's test?

I remember the first time we had met Uncle Early and Aunt Sylvia. It was when they stayed in Virginia at the hospital with Sam's mother. She was Uncle Early's sister and we could see he loved her very much. Those two weeks while we waited for Truly to pass, we got a Bible lesson every day and we loved how they taught. We could feel the love vibrating off of them for God and we craved for more of that teaching. They spoke about God like he really was God. Like nothing was impossible with God. Our job was to only believe it. We didn't have to die to meet him or hear him, or for him to hear us. We could have a personal relationship with this God every day. We could talk to God and he would talk back to us, like a real father did. He takes care of us and loves us, like a real mama does. They were the reason we all decided to move to Jacksonville. All of us wanted to know this God, their God.

You say, what does all that have to do with an impossible birth? Everything! It was their teaching that taught us how to stand on God's promises. That God loves to bless all of us. Not just a few. He may use only a few, but he blesses the just and the unjust. That everything that had life in it was God flowing, and God would never curse himself. He said the curses came from negative thinking, ignorance. God's people died physical deaths because they lacked knowledge in life. He blesses all. Jesus had come to earth and resurrected and went back to God, proving there is no such thing as death. Death was a lie, the figment of flesh imaginations. God hears everyone that speaks because he lives inside of every living thing. He will give us a baby because we believe he will, in his own timing, in his own way.

Ignorance had almost destroyed these kids and we knew we all needed a fresh start. Aunt Sylvia and Uncle Early were our anchors, our new journey that would lead us away from pain and grief. They knew they had their work cut out with all of us, too. That is why we ran to them about Tammy's problem. We knew if anyone had an answer or knew what to do about Tammy, they would know.

Yes, we had tested their faith daily since we had moved to Jacksonville, and our trust in them was growing. They had proved they believed what they spoke and preached to us. We had been fooled by religion because of our own ignorance and wrong teaching. So we walked on these new waters very carefully. They weren't like the people that quoted a verse in the Bible and called themselves saved. Living the flesh life six days a week and on Sunday acting and talking like a Christian. Fakes, the blind leading the blind to death, they said. With each day that passed we witnessed their joy in the Lord, and we learned a little more about God's true love.

Their way of teaching the Word in Faith was in every game we played. They loved to play dice and with every number that came up, he quoted a Bible verse and asked, "Do you know the meaning of that?" Everything they did had a Bible lesson in it. The loving and joking ways made us ask questions. Some nights we would be at their house until after 2 a.m., wishing we weren't tired and wishing we didn't have school and work the next day. They taught God in such a way that we believed we could ask and receive anything, including a baby. They taught us the Supernatural God who does the impossible. "Not gonna do," they would say, "but does every moment do the impossible. Nothing was too great or too small for this God."

After three years or more in Jacksonville, a bond of trust grew deeper and deeper. God had become our God in words and deeds. We had a burning in our stomach; Uncle Early said that was the soul that was on fire to know the meaning of every word Jesus spoke. How many times had Jesus said it? Who was he speaking it to? How did it make you feel when you read that? They would ask. They were giving us homework without even saying the word homework. Their vibrations of love and joy filled any house they entered. They said Jesus did his work and finished it. Now it was time for us to manifest Christ just like He manifested the Father God. Just being around them made us feel loved, special, happy, and full of hope.

Aunt Sylvia loved to cook and we all loved to eat. She played her role as the great cook to bait us over or invite them over to our house. Feeding our crowd was a job in itself. So we knew God had to have her to do it, or she would have run in the other direction. They loved to see us all eat, and we could put away some food. Her love for God and for us to grow in God was so deep that she never complained, but called it an honor and a privilege. That was the bait that hooked us all in the beginning, her delicious cooking. Eating that good physical and spiritual food hooked us all on the word of God. We became just as hungry for God's word as we were for her cooking. They worked as a team like a musical band in tune, in rhythm with each word and deed. Aunt Sylvia knew every key to Uncle Early's moves, from when to get the Bible to prove a point, to when to speak up and help him out in quoting a verse. And so every opportunity for them was a chance to feed God's little souls the living food to help them grow in God. "When I see God in you, well, I'm alright," they would say.

Over at their house every day or they at ours, always doing everything together. They took our soul development seriously. "With food and fellowship," Uncle Early said, "that's how Jesus won the multitude." If it hadn't been for them teaching us how to walk and talk and believe by faith daily and believe in God's word, I don't believe there would have been a dream or a baby. They truly were the anchors that held us up until we could stand alone.

I was determined to stay focused on God and wait for proof that He heard us. I became overwhelmed with faith. Hope grew with every waking hour that God would give us a baby. Every night I would take out my Bible and read about Abraham and Sarah. How God gave them a baby when he was a hundred years old and she was ninety years old. Sometimes to Sam out loud and sometimes silently I read. We laughed about their age, and Sam would remark, "Wouldn't that be something if God reversed your surgery and gave us a baby boy." My reply was always, "No! That wouldn't be something. That would be a disaster. Tammy wants a baby. Let's just stick to that hope and plan." Then we would kiss and roll over to go to sleep.

CHAPTER TWO

THE FIRST DREAM

CHAPTER TWO

THE FIRST DREAM

A month or so had passed and we didn't speak of what the doctor said. Only what Aunt Sylvia and Uncle Early had told us to say, "God is working on it."

All of us had resumed our normal lives with church, school, work, football, movies, skating, bowling, cookouts, eat-outs, the beach, sleepovers, etc. Just what every American family does, until the night the dream came to me.

In this dream, I could see myself lying in bed asleep when Gabriel the archangel appeared. Whether in a trance or not, I didn't know. What I do know is I was witnessing the whole scene. I could see the room and every picture on the wall. The bathroom door, the sink in it, even the mirror on the wall above the sink. I could see the headboard and footboard of the bed as well as the color of the blanket. I could even see Sam lying beside me. Every detail of the room from ceiling to floor, this huge magnificent angel and myself was clear as crystal.

Had I left my body? Was I having an out-of-body experience? I felt like I had known this angel all my life. I could see his radiance and how it flowed from him. His presence filled the whole room with radiant golden, blue, green, yellow and white light. With just enough purple in the room that made you feel you were in a King's palace.

Then suddenly what had appeared as my lifeless body just sat up in bed, eyes wide opened and starring straight at this huge Archangel standing at the foot of my bed. It was like I was seeing from inside of my body, yet outside of it. Then as I watched, I witnessed him walk over to my bed. The Light that flowed from him became more beautiful with each step. The warmth from him felt like the sun beaming down on me on a July afternoon. So many colors of light that a rainbow wouldn't give it justice. Some I knew, and some were so glorious. They sparkled like rubies and diamonds all over the room, like snow falling, except magnifying glorious colors. Some of the white ones looked like pure opals and pearls. The most beautiful sapphire colors in blue that they just took my breath away. The greens and amber yellows looked like shining stars as they moved in the air and all around the room. What did it all mean? I thought to myself as I absorbed all this beauty.

Then he looked straight at me. His eyes met mine and suddenly I was in a calm, quiet state in my mind and I could feel it throughout my body. He never moved his head to the left or to the right. He just stared straight into my eyes. Yet in all that radiance, I could feel fear rise up from the lower parts of my belly within me. Suddenly I was aware of everything that was going on inside my body.

Then my whole body began to shake. It felt like an earthquake as my teeth rattled. It felt like fear was holding on, but the force was too strong. Slowly, like pushing a heavy wagon uphill, I could feel fear losing its grip. The space at the bottom of my belly was now empty and light, like a fresh spring rain had just fell upon the earth. But just that space felt that way.

The remainder of my belly area and chest felt heavy, dark and gloomy where the fear still had a strong hold. I even felt my spirit trying to scream for help. As I watched this heavenly being come closer, the shaking grew stronger. With each shake, fear lost ground. The clean fresh air rose higher within me. The higher fear rose, the easier I could feel the joy behind it pushing it up. Every inch of ground that joy occupied felt clean. Something more powerful inside of me was removing the fear step by step.

Was it the Father God form or the Holy Spirit form or Jesus? I didn't have a clue and didn't care. With each step he took I could feel the joy rising up and becoming stronger as it owned the space where fear had once occupied. From the pit of my belly up inside of me I could feel fear being pushed closer to my mouth. When the fear reached my throat, I felt like I was choking. I grabbed my throat and tried to speak. All I wanted to do was scream for Jesus. Jesus help me, I heard my mind say, but no words came out. Please Jesus help me. I felt like fear would win and choke me to death. I could feel my throat closing up and death's grip on it. I couldn't breathe. Help me, I could hear myself inside saying, but it was like help wasn't coming. I could see this archangel Gabriel standing over me. I could feel his eyes like fire staring. His radiance overwhelmed me as this battle between fear and joy took place within me. I heard myself with my mind say, "Why won't you help me?"

Then suddenly his power overwhelmed me, and what seem like a mighty force pushed me back onto the bed. My head rested on the pillow as I felt that calm, relaxing energy flow through me. I could see what looked like a white figure of light. I could feel how powerful he really was. He had my full attention. Joy had filled my whole being. All the heaviness I had felt was lifted up out of me. My mind actually felt clean, clear and pure, like it had been washed. As I laid on the bed feeling like I had been washed inside and out and ready for a quiet little nap, he spoke.

"Have no fear. I am Gabriel. This night you will conceive a son and his name will be Joseph."

Then like he blended into the air invisible, yet with his presence all around, I drifted off to sleep in a place of silence. A place that appeared to be like pure nothingness to rest my whole being, I was conscious yet resting like a baby. In this place, I rested with a calm and peaceful environment all around me, like I was asleep yet awake.

When I actually woke up I was back in my physical bed. Whether I had been in my body or out of my body during the night, I know not. But it was early in the morning and he had disappeared as quickly as he had appeared. His presence lingered in the room as I lay there and pondered over what had happened to me during the night.

Was I going to have a baby? What did it mean? The story pertaining to Gabriel in the New Testament where he came and spoke to Elizabeth's husband and told him his wife would have a son and his name was John. Another time when he appeared to Mary and told her she would have a son and his name was

Jesus. Was it the answer we had prayed for, for Tammy? It certainly meant something, and it was from God, I was certain of that.

I could see the beautiful sun shining in our bedroom window and it appeared more beautiful than ever before. Every detail was resting in my clean heart and mind. The joy overwhelmed me.

I jumped up and ran to the living room to catch everyone before they left for school and work, yelling, "Wait! Wait! Guess what I dreamed?" So excited I could barely get the words out.

Almost out of the door, they stopped, turned around, and looked at me like I had lost my mind. They didn't realize how close to the truth they were, for I had lost my old mind and had a brand new mind.

The details of the dream poured out and off my lips like someone else had spoken them through me. Just like the river had flowed in my mind during the night, the words flowed. I watched their expression change from morning moodiness to joy and belief, like the words spoken were magic, and turned them all into a ball of joy. Awesome!

Wendy shouted, "Its Tammy! It's Tammy! She's gonna have a baby and it's a boy."

Tammy stood in total shock, so it appeared. She was speechless for sure. While Wendy, Nell and Penny jumped up and down, holding hands and dancing around her shouting, "Tammy is having a baby. Tammy is having a baby. Don't you see, Tammy? God has given His answer. You're gonna have a baby boy, just like Mary and Jesus."

Then suddenly Penny stopped dancing and reached over and hugged Tammy. I saw her tears of joy flowing like that same river as she held onto Tammy. They stood arm in arm and just held each other and let the tears flow. That same joy I had experienced in the dream filled the whole room. A house of joy!

Wendy saw her daddy coming up the hall and screamed out, "Daddy, Tammy is gonna have a baby. A boy! Carolyn had a dream. Tell him, Carolyn. Tell daddy the dream."

"A boy," Sammy said in his loud, bossy voice. "That's good. Are you kids going to school?" He was headed out of the kitchen door with his lunch box in his hand for work.

Everyone turned around to look at the clock and realized the time. They ran out of the front door for the school bus that was already waiting for them. Penny yelled back, "Mama, can we tell our friends now?"

"Yes," I yelled back.

Tammy was still speechless as she entered her school bus for work. She gave me one glance with eyes full of tears that said thank you with a smile.

Shouting praises to God as I ran down the hall into my private bathroom ripping clothes off, I jumped in for a quick shower and threw some make up on and ran out to the Lincoln, brushing my hair. No cell phones at the time, so getting to work this day was a joyous twenty-five miles downtown to Jacksonville.

As soon as I got to my office, I called Aunt Sylvia and Uncle Early to tell them about the dream. They were calm, but sure God had decided and the answer had come.

Then I went into Mrs. Bray's office to tell her God had answered our prayer. She was my boss and the wife of one of the owners of the law firm. Yet she had more compassion than any woman I had ever met on a job, especially for a boss. She impressed me the first day I went to work there. I always felt she was the backbone of that company. She had a deep understanding of her employees' needs. Her compassion when problems arose with their children. When the drama of life meant leaving work early or showing up late, she just listened and said, "If you need us, call us."

She amazed me with all her responsibilities at work as well as home. So telling her was like sharing with a friend rather than a boss. We worked in a stress-free environment because of her. She never considered anyone late unless there was an important meeting we had to attend and showed up late. Any other time, she allowed us to stay over and get our eight hours and our work done.

So walking in her office at 10 a.m. just meant I would be there until 6 p.m. She always seem just as interested in hearing about our children's problems and happy events as she was in sharing her own.

Mrs. Bray looked up from her desk as I stood knocking at her door and motioned for me to enter. She immediately saw my joyful face and bursting from the seams with joy. "Carolyn, do you have good news for me today?" she asked.

My mouth opened and the words flooded out of me again like a river. She looked in shock for about a second with her mouth hung opened, and then jumped on the intercom and announced, "Listen up, people, Carolyn is going to be a grandmother. Let's stop and give God thanks for a second, and then back to work." Then she stood up and gave me a very strong and sure hug and said, "Keep me posted. Now go to work and make us some money."

When I turned to leave her office, everyone was standing to give me a hug and a few words of encouragement. They had walked this with me since the day Tammy came home with the news from the doctor's office. They had stood with us in prayer and believed as we had for God's will to be done, and we hoped it was to give Tammy a baby. Most of them had children from newborn to teens to adults, and knew all about the daily drama that went on in a household with them. If there were any non-believers working in that company, they must not have worked in our department. A glorious place where we could work, worship, fellowship and still make money. One big happy family!

God had proven to us that he does hear our prayers. He had proven to us, like Aunt Sylvia and Uncle Early had said, that he does talk to us and he cares about us. That dream was only the first step. Now we had to wait for a baby to be conceived. That was the next step. Conception!

When I shared with some friends at the community church we attended because of the youth program, they said it was my imagination. They were right! I accepted as truth that dreams and visions were real. That imagination is a gift from God. Each person has his or her own idea. I hold as my opinion that some people dream about bad things happening, and some dream only good stuff. I have a firm conviction in the reality of dreams and visions.

But I believe all dreams are good, even when they seem bad.

What evidence do we have that dreams come true? Only people. How can we tell when they are telling the truth? We wait. Jesus said, "I tell you these things before they happen, so when they happen, you will know it was I telling you."

I see and listen to people say all the time, "I knew that was going to happen." But that is not what Jesus said. Jesus said, "I will show you or tell you these things before they happen, so you will know that it is I that have spoken with you." The word 'before' is the key in that statement. That's why I believe and know that I know nothing unless He tells me or shows me first.

I feel that all credit goes to a higher energy, and I just happen to sense that is God the Father, God the Mother and God the Son, the LORD Jesus Christ. They are all three, yet one person. Like me, I am spirit living in a body possessing a soul. I am three yet one. Maybe to have a firm conviction in the reality of something, we all need to experience it in dreams and visions. Some call it mentally alert or awake. Some say we must intentionally say and think something is real to make it real. But then, who makes us believe that?

People say, "Be forever cool," but they don't know if it will be. But when God says, "Be forever cool," he means it. Maybe that is why I believe, think, feel, and know.

I began having dreams at the age of nine, dreams that came true. At that time I didn't pray for anything special. I just prayed like other people in the family, the same standard prayer. But one day my Uncle Press was very sick, and doctors said he was going to die. I could see how worried and upset my Aunt Ellen and cousin Johnny were and had no way to help them. That night I prayed and asked Jesus if he would show me if he was going to die or live. Then I went off to sleep. But while sleeping I saw Uncle Press in my dreams, and he was riding in Johnny's car coming towards home. Then I woke up. So I ran in the kitchen and told daddy that Uncle Press wasn't going to die. He was coming home from the hospital. Then I skipped off to play.

Another time he was sick and in the hospital and again Jesus showed me he was coming home. After awhile I started to see that when I felt someone else's pain or cared about others, it touched my heart and made me sad. Then Jesus showed me the answer in a dream and made me happy again.

When I was a teenager I wanted to date, so I asked Jesus to send me a boyfriend. One that would marry me, and I would have his babies. In a dream Jesus showed me a young man with cold black hair, deep dark blue eyes and tan skin. I saw his smile and fell in love with him at first sight. Sure enough, a few years later I was on the school bus going to school and saw him working at the gas station. My heart leaped for joy when I saw him. I hadn't even met him yet, but I loved him.

I don't know if other people's dreams came true when they didn't ask Jesus. I asked some people, and most didn't even believe in dreams and visions. All I knew was that in our Southern Baptist church, my teacher said all we had to do was pray to Jesus and His Father and Mother God, and anything we wanted He would give to us.

I just believed daddy when he told us that God is with us all the time and he knows everything. All I needed to do is ask and he gives me the answers. It may not be the answer we want, but it will be the right answer every time.

I believe God is like my daddy and mother. When I am sad I run to him, and he cheers me up. When I am hurting, he comforts me while I heal. Sometimes like mama and daddy, he says later. Guess what? When later came, so did what I asked for. "I can only do as my father does," Jesus said.

He loves helping people. He loves making his children happy. What more can I say? I believe we have dreams and visions, and God makes sure they all come to pass because he gives them.

CHAPTER THREE

THE SECOND DREAM

CHAPTER THREE

THE SECOND DREAM

The first day had certainly been filled with excitement and joy from the first dream. By bedtime my mind was exhausted as well as my body. The house was still filled with joy and the kids were busy with homework and fighting over the phone (yes, that was before cell phones). So I decided to retire to the bedroom for a little relaxation in hopes I would fall asleep early. I was hoping the silence I had experienced the night before was still lingering in there as I propped my pillows up to read the Bible before actually giving into a little television time and sleep.

I wanted to read the story of Gabriel coming to Mother Mary and announcing Jesus' birth again. Not that I thought I was anyone special like her or anything. I just felt I must feel what she felt the night Gabriel came to her and announced the birth of her male child. She could help me out here, since she experienced all this before I did. I wanted to see it again and try to find other places in the Bible where Gabriel had showed up. But it wasn't but a few minutes before I slipped off into dream world again.

Whether in my body or out of it I know not. I was in this peaceful, restful place again. Gabriel was with me and in his radiant white robe, beaming with pink, blue, and golden rays flowing from him. This time his radiance seemed more beautiful than before. He had more rainbow colors around him. His warmth seemed deeper this time and his presence didn't frighten me. Actually I was excited to see him, like we had known each other for eternity. I waited in excitement as he walked toward me from the door entrance. My whole being was jumping up and down inside like butterflies and jellybeans. He slowly walked in his calm self and just like the night before he stopped at the foot of my bed and stared straight at me. Again, like the night before, he was clearing my mind of trash and left it flowing like a pure river in a calm state.

Then he showed me Tammy's birth, but instead of it being Tammy it was I actually experiencing the event. I was in labor and having a hard time giving birth. I could see the stress and pain on my face as I pushed. I felt exhaustion and the terrifying pain. I actually could feel it, like it was myself, giving birth to this baby. I felt God was pulling this baby straight from my loins. I could see Gabriel with his hands turning the baby inside of me, and the pain was almost unbearable. I saw how I fell back onto the bed to relax a second, only to push and scream once more. All I could focus on was getting this baby out of me. I would collapse back onto the bed again and catch my breath, only to rise within a second to scream and push again. My face was burning with sweat. This baby was taking all the strength I had within me.

I saw Gabriel stand up in his white robe over me as I endured the pain in silence. All I could think about was the pain, because that was all I could feel. My God, I thought I would die and even hoped I would. It blinded me to see much of anything after that or hear anything.

The room was a gray smoky color and very still. The doctors and nurses moved in slow motion. Whatever was happening to me, I didn't have a clue. It was a long and painful dream. Hours went by and the pain had not ceased, nor had the baby come. Sweat poured down my face like boiling tea. Pushing and screaming over and over as Gabriel just stood there.

Why won't he help me? I thought. Why won't he let them give me a c-section or something for the pain? Why do I have to suffer like this?

Finally the baby was born and Gabriel announced, "It's a boy, and his name shall be Joseph."

I saw the baby boy as the nurse took him. He had blue eyes and blond hair. Long, slender, funny looking feet like something was wrong with his toes, and long fingers, as I watched with such intensity to see all of him. Then Gabriel disappeared as before and it faded away.

When I awoke from this dream, I was confused, yet full of joy like I had felt each time after one of my own babies had been born. Was it I having this baby or Tammy? I was completely worn out. My body felt like it had been run over by a Mack truck, as they say. I looked at the clock and realized I had been in that dream five hours or more.

Still the middle of the night, I laid there and thanked God for giving Tammy this baby boy. As confused as I was, I knew we had prayed for Tammy to have a baby, not me. I thanked him for allowing me to see, hear, and feel Gabriel, and experience this event in a dream before it happened. The dreams made me feel like this child was mine already. I knew I couldn't have any more children but also knew God worked the impossible and anything was possible. But it was Tammy that wanted a baby, not me. I wanted her to be happy and receive from God what she wanted, so with that thought I rolled over and hugged Sam and fell back to sleep.

The next morning it amazed me how quickly I had fallen back to sleep after a five-hour labor and delivery experience in my dream. I jumped to my feet and ran to Tammy's room to tell her the news. I knew Sam and Tony had already left for work. I just left out the part about the painful delivery. She replied, "That's good, Mama, but I'll be glad when I am actually pregnant."

I knew what she was saying. It was May 13th when the doctors told her the tests results, and we were already in the month of June. I felt she was thinking it was all part of my own imagination, but I couldn't stop believing now.

I called Aunt Sylvia and she said it was God confirming that Tammy would give birth to a healthy baby boy, but have a difficult delivery. When I asked her about my confusion, she said we were all one in God and God was allowing me to experience this in a dream, because Tammy didn't have enough faith to believe for herself. She said there was no need for prayer. God had showed us she would conceive and give birth, and what type of birth she would have. She said we needed to thank God for the pregnancy and healthy birth of this male child. And that we needed to pray for strength and peace of mind now. That she would tell Uncle Early and the ladies at church and see what they say. That she would get back to me later. In the meantime, she said, just tell Tammy to hold onto the dream. Not to allow any other thoughts to enter her mind. But that she will conceive and give birth to a healthy baby boy, and continue to thank God and praise him.

I returned to Tammy's room and reported what Aunt Sylvia had said. She nodded as she finished dressing for work, and I shut her door and went to do the same.

At work that day I only shared with one friend, Pat. She was a preacher's wife and was used to hearing all sorts of things, and didn't judge anything. She agreed with Aunt Sylvia, and so to my office I went.

The whole day all I could think about was that blue-eyed, blond-haired baby boy we would be receiving in nine months. I felt Tammy actually conceived that night while I was having the dream. Trying to get work done was the most difficult thing to do that day. It was the most difficult day I had ever had at work. I just couldn't concentrate. I kept hearing one client after another say, "Are you listening?" Finally, I just gathered my things and went to tell my boss I was headed home. I needed to pray and just be alone awhile. She asked out of concern if she could help, but I knew she couldn't. I just shook my head and tears filled my eyes as I turned and walked out.

I drove very slowly home, listening to a preacher on the radio. He was confirming also. I knew it was God talking to me through him. That preacher didn't know me in the physical, and I didn't know him. He kept saying over and over, "Hold onto that dream. You got to hold onto that dream. Never let it go. Just hold onto to that dream. Give God praise. for He has heard your prayer."

Tears of joy flowed down my face for the blue-eyed baby boy about to be born in our family. Yet there was sorrow in my heart for Tammy and her painful delivery.

Before I got in the house, the kids were asking me why I came home so early. I just said I was very tired and needed some rest.

Wendy asked me if I'd had any more dreams. When I told them yes I had, and Tammy gave birth to a healthy boy with blue eyes and blond hair, all they could say was he will look like you, then.

They were happy, chatting to each other while running for the phone that was ringing. Me, thinking it was for one of the teens, I went on to the bathroom. But instead it was Aunt Sylvia calling to invite us to supper around 6:30 p.m. She said she had called the office and my secretary had told her I had left for the day.

"Oh glory," I shouted, "I didn't want to cook anyway." I knew they wanted to help us encourage Tammy to hold onto the dream and watch her thoughts and wait for the manifestation to come to pass. I also knew I had two hours to rest as I lay across my bed.

My body felt the same as it did the day after I had given birth to Tammy years ago. I could feel the softness of the mattress as it hugged itself around me. Since the Archangel Gabriel had appeared in that room, it had become my favorite place to hide from the world and all its problems. Like his presence had filled the whole room with a radiant peace, and just entering it made me relax and fall asleep.

6: 00 p.m. came and time to pack up the car and head to Aunt Sylvia's for dinner and fellowship. Tammy and Tony didn't mind as long as we ate somewhere besides their house.

Just as I had suspected, they wanted to encourage us all, but especially Tammy and Tony, to hold onto the dreams. During dinner Aunt Sylvia opened the conversation with Daniel 8:16, "Gabriel, tell this man the meaning of the vision/dream." Then she proceeded to Daniel 9:21 and read, "While I was still asleep, Gabriel, the angel I had seen in the previous dream came to me again, and said, 'as soon as you began to pray, an answer was given, which I have come to tell you, for you are highly esteemed. Therefore, consider the message and understand the vision.'"

Then Aunt Sylvia continued to explain to us, but speaking directly to Tammy. That God heard our prayer to give Tammy a baby, a healthy baby boy. And God had sent His own archangel with the message in a dream to your mother, Tammy. Now you must do your part, she said. You must be watchful of your thoughts. Think only about the message and thank God for sending the answer. When the carnal mind brings you thoughts of doubt, you must replace them with thoughts of the dream and thank God. We all will wait with you. But just as surely as we all sit at this table, it will come to pass.

Uncle Early added his comments to say that it was more than just a dream and a baby. That it was a sign from God for this generation. He continued, This baby would be the sign for his generation. He will be born Christ-like and his very presence would vibrate God. For God has chosen you, Tammy, to conceive a baby the same way Mother Mary conceived Jesus our Savior. There are many women in this generation, your generation, that will be visited by the angel and announce the conception and birth of God's light children upon the earth. It's time for the Living Spoken Word to come forth out of these temples. The very fact that you are the one we have prayed for proves that you are a sign for your generation, like Mary was to hers. God is revealing himself to you and this generation, and is proving he is God to this generation. The fact God has chosen this generation, your generation will see many changes. The next twenty years will bring forth more change than any other time in history. Some good and some not so good, but needed for soul development. For some they will be good, but for others they will seem like a curse. This male child will be loved by positive people and hated by the negative crowd. Some will adore him and others will be insanely jealous and envious of him. Like Christ he will walk among the darkness but the darkness will not touch him. This too is God's will. He will live a blessed life, surrounded by family and friends that love and adore him. Beware of Delia, for she will come out of jealousy and envy to steal his joy and destroy his good name. Praise God for allowing me to live long enough in this body to see this day. For he spoke of the children of light being born, now it is time and will be.

Fear caught our hearts and Tammy began to cry. But Uncle Early ignored our looks of fear and our tears by looking down to his King James Bible lying in his lap and proceeded to read Luke 1:19. "The angel Gabriel answered, 'I am Gabriel. I stand in the presence of God, and I have been sent to speak to you and to tell you this good news. Believe my words, which will come true at the proper time.'" Then he skipped down to verse 26. "Greetings, you are highly favored! The LORD is with you. Do not be afraid. You have found favor with God."

Then he stopped reading, closed his Bible and looked straight at Tammy and added, do as the Bible says, have no fear. This male child will be born in God's will, will live in God's will and will die according to God's will. So put all thoughts out of your mind but this one. God has chosen you to bring forth a male child his way, a sign for his generation. God's angels will protect him as long as he walks this earth. He will have no fear of death, for he will not know death as some know it. To you and the world he will seem to be any ordinary child, but to God he is a sign for this generation.

After all that, like he had prophesied to us, we had many questions but he answered none. Uncle Early said, "Only believe." That God didn't show him how long this male child would live on earth or the answer to any of the questions we had asked. But only what he shared was what God had revealed unto him. Our job was to believe the dreams as they had come. It would come to pass. If it weren't of God, it would come to nothing. For all things that are anything is just God. There is nothing else.

Silence filled the house as we got up to wash dishes and put food away. Uncle Early and Sam left for the den to watch television. I asked Aunt Sylvia a few questions, but she enforced the same by saying only believe. She did ask me if I knew that Early couldn't read. When I replied I didn't know that, she laughed and said, "God taught him how to read the Bible word for word. Now he just knows it word for word." Then she started singing the song, 'Only Believe' and we all joined in.

After dinner and dishes we usually played dice, but this night we all just wanted to go home. Our minds were on the words Uncle Early had spoken to us and we just wanted to go home. A sign for this generation rang out in the car, but none of us knew what it meant.

CHAPTER FOUR

THE THIRD DREAM

CHAPTER FOUR

THE THIRD DREAM

Once home from Aunt Sylvia's and getting things ready for morning, I retired to my bedroom. I reached for my NIV bible and opened it to Luke 1:19 and began to read out loud. "I am Gabriel. I stand in the presence of God. I have been sent to speak to you and to tell you this good news. Believe my words, which will come true at their proper time." I read those verses again and again and prayed for understanding. As I read them aloud, Sam came in and suggested we lay it all on the shelf and just go to sleep. He agreed with Uncle Early and added we think too much. Just leave it alone and go to sleep, as he climbed in bed on his side.

I got dressed for bed and climbed in behind him. With the television on as usual, I fell asleep in short order. How long I had been asleep I don't know, or if I was in my body or out of it. But one thing I do know, I entered the dream world again like before. The angel Gabriel entered my bedroom in all white with a golden glow around him and spoke unto me these words.

"Greetings, you who are highly favored! The Lord is with you. Do not be afraid, Carolyn. You have found favor with God. You will take the male child and move to Virginia. A job will be provided for you. His earthly mama and daddy will follow. He will be great and will be the presence of God manifested to all God. His smile will melt hearts that are cold and hard as stone. The Holy Spirit will come upon you and the power of the Most High will overshadow you. So the Holy Spirit will be with him to witness through him. To the world he will appear as an ordinary boy, but his presence will tell them he is not ordinary. The time is fifteen months from his birth date that you will take him to Virginia and surround him with family. Fear not, for God will open the doors for you in the proper time."

Then he waved his arms and I saw a little boy about fifteen months old climbing up on my coffee table and jumping off with his cowboy boots and guns on. This little boy jumped up and off several times. and his smile was as Gabriel had said. Eyes that sparkled like stars and his presence powerful as a magnet. His smile vibrated joy and his surroundings were as peaceful as a calm lake.

My heart burned with love as I watched him play. I wanted to grab him, hold him next to my heart. I already loved him. Let me kiss him all over. He drew my heart with such force I just knew I would touch him. Like a strong magnet he drew me. Just to touch him and hold him in my arms. Just to feel him next to my skin. But just as I reached to pick him up, I woke up and the dream vanished. The dream remained very much alive within me, but the visual was gone.

I wasn't sure what to say or who to tell when I awoke from this dream. It was no use in trying to go back to sleep. I just laid in the silence and pondered over the dream, the words, what I saw and what I was feeling. The excitement was overwhelming me. I wondered who this baby really belonged to. Was it Tammy's or mine? Was he everybody's baby? Was he born with the personality and character of Jesus? I remembered second Corinthians two, where it says we are workers together with God. What kind of life would he really have on this earth? Was this the way God looked at every birth? His word says children are a blessing from God.

For thousands of years people had been speculating about the nature of dreams, were they real or not? Yet within myself I knew they were real. At least the ones I had already had that had come to pass. Somehow I knew these three dreams were real and would come to pass.

What confused me was, why me? But the Lord within answered that one by saying, why not you? Then I remembered, was it because I had loved God's word since I heard about Jesus at age six?

Daddy's words came to me. "Carolyn, God is always watching and listening, so never do anything in the dark that you don't want exposed in the light."

I also remembered from the story how Joseph's brothers in the Bible hated him. That scared me to think my family or anyone would hate this baby. Then I remembered how people hated Jesus and he asked them, for what good deed do you want to kill me? All my thoughts were making me afraid. I convinced myself that God gave this baby, and he would protect him also.

This dream was different. The first dream reminded me of the conception of Jesus. The second dream reminded me of Jesus's birth. But this dream reminded me of when the angel went to Joseph and told him to take the baby Jesus to another town for his protection. I pondered all these things in my mind. Did the evil forces know who he was when we didn't even know that ourselves? Even in Jesus's story, the remainder of his childhood was a mystery because it wasn't written in my Bible. So it made me wonder if God had chosen the same for this baby named Joseph. We asked for a baby boy for Tammy, and all of this was taking me on a spiritual journey that I didn't even understand.

I remembered the words of John where Jesus said, "You do not understand what I'm doing, but later on you will understand."

The sun was up and time to get up and get teens off to school and the men off to work, along with Tammy and myself. I didn't know what to do with this dream. I hoped no one would ask if I'd had another dream. I knew Tammy had already gotten tired of waiting for the conception. Telling her we would be moving in fifteen months from his birth was just too much at this time. Thank God everyone was running late so the subject didn't come up.

After I got to work I ran over to Pat's desk to tell her about the dream and asked her what God was up to. She was just as confused as I was. She said, just trust. And pray for God's will be done. With that, I left her office.

That afternoon I rode by Aunt Sylvia and Uncle Early's house to share the dream with them and asked their thoughts on it. Uncle Early was at Sam's shop, so Aunt Sylvia and I talked. I could see from the expression on her face that was not what she wanted to hear. I asked if they would consider moving also. I didn't want to leave them or the ministry. But she stated they would never leave Jacksonville, Florida. That was where God had them in ministry. But I had to obey God also.

She did share that I may have misunderstood the dream and we might not move. That it could mean something different, and we would have to wait and see.

On the way home I was listening to Kenneth Hagin on the radio. He kept repeating, "Whatever God tells you to do, do it without haste and be not afraid." I could feel his words awaken inside me. Like the sun, they burned in my heart. I felt it was God speaking directly to me through him. Flashbacks of the words from the dream 'be not afraid' and the burning in my heart reminded me to just trust God. Leave it alone and let God do whatever he pleased. I continued to listen, fighting my own thoughts so his words could enter. I pulled up in my driveway. I barely remembered driving home, like I had been in a trance or something.

A whole month had passed and still no conception. School was out and we had planned our trip to Virginia. The Smith reunion was always on the first Sunday in June and we were excited about seeing everyone. The kids knew they would stay, and Sam and I knew we would have a month to ourselves. No kids! We looked forward to some alone time. Tammy worked for the school system and could go with us. Tony, well, he would just take off work like Sam did or stay and live without Tammy for two weeks. He knew she was still a mama's girl and he loved that. He didn't try to interfere, but just blended in the experience, even called me Ma. He enjoyed that because he knew I hated being called that.

The end of summer vacation was over and we were back in Virginia, visiting and picking up the kids to return to Florida. The trip back to Jacksonville was not as much fun as it was going to Virginia. The kids were sad and cranky. All were homesick before we got out of the state and in that 'don't touch me' mood. That would last until we got out of North Carolina, or until Sam and I couldn't take any more.

Life goes on whether we like it or not!

CHAPTER FIVE

THE GOOD NEWS

CHAPTER FIVE

THE GOOD NEWS

The end of July 1988 revealed some exciting news. Tammy hadn't told anyone but her mama that she had missed her period. She was so afraid she would jinx it that she kept it to herself, until she had test results from her doctor.

On July 21st, 1988, she held the proof in her hands as she ran in the house with the results. Her smile covered her face as she shook the positive results that proved she was pregnant. Her smile had already given her away. The test was the proof that she needed to convince everyone else.

The greatest day in our life was when God proved the dreams were from him. Tony didn't stop smiling. He just stood there and let Tammy have the glory, sharing with us. His smile told us he was about to jump out of his pants. The energy that he vibrated was spreading to us very quickly.

Wendy, Penny and Nell kept asking if she was sure as they looked at the test for themselves. I was crying, just seeing the test in her hand was enough for me. So much joy poured from me, I couldn't even speak. Sam's look of surprise made him speechless. But he was the first to jump on the phone to call Aunt Sylvia and Uncle Early. Then he shouted back, "They're on their way."

I started counting on my fingers as to when she had conceived to compare it with the dreams. From her last period, she had conceived somewhere around June 21st, 1988, one month from the first dream. We had his due date as March 21st, 1989. No more doubts. God had given those dreams. We all bathed in the good news and went out to celebrate over dinner as Sam's treat. Then Tony and Tammy went to his grandparents and his sisters.

The next day the excitement was so overwhelming we had to shop. First thing on the list was a movie camera. We had to film every day of the pregnancy, every doctor's appointment, the baby shower, the growth of Joseph inside her belly, right up to labor and delivery. By the end of that day we were exhausted. No dinner prepared for Tony, Sam or the kids. Sam came in the back door and saw that the table was full of floor plans, paint samples, magazines of curtains, baby beds and all the trimmings, plus a new movie camera, but no dinner.

"What's this? Where's the food? Baby or no baby, we need to eat," he said. Tony shook his head in agreement. Then he looked at me and said, "Did you bother to go to work today?" Then Sam turned to Tony and said, "Damn, Tony, I guess we will have to feed ourselves and everyone else, plus this baby coming," as he went out of the back door. But Tony stayed behind, kissed Tammy and said, "Hey Ma. Did you have fun today?" Knowing that we had.

We quickly cleared the table and proceeded to cook supper. The plans and design of Joseph's room and bed would be blue with clouds. We had already agreed on that.

A few days later, Tammy went to her doctor. He started sharing his doubts as to whether she would carry this baby full term or not, and he told her that he already foresaw problems. That he would set her up with specialists that could handle them.

But when she asked. what problems? He stated, "To start with, there is every medical reason for you not to be pregnant. Yet here you are pregnant. I don't have an explanation for that." Then he exited the room while Tammy waited for the arrangements to be made.

Later that day she came by my office and shared. I noticed she didn't have an ounce of fear. She flowed with it all like she was led by an angel or an unseen being. Pat said she floated like the air was carrying her. The doctor's scientific expert advice or opinions didn't matter to Tammy anymore. God was the boss and only God in this matter, as she hugged Tammy. Then she asked, did you tell him about the dreams?

No. Tammy said the expression on his face when he saw the health department test, and later after he looked at his own test results, told me he didn't believe what he saw with his own eyes, so why tell him about the dreams? Tammy stated that her pregnancy started with God and would end with God.

With God driving this ship, she had a wonderful pregnancy. We experienced every inch of this journey every day with her. Tammy glowed like a lighthouse at night overlooking the ocean. Her smile was plastered on her face every day, as well as Tony's and ours. We knew her every pain and Joseph's every kick. We took notes for his baby book and movies of almost everything. We watched and made sure she didn't overwork herself. We shared in every doctor or hospital visit, shared in the joy of every gift and every comment. We had her work place and mine as support. As well as two churches and all the families and friends that knew about the dreams. We thanked God every day that she had no complications. And she had none during the whole pregnancy.

One day we got a phone call. Tony had wrecked their car on interstate 95. The car was totaled. He was fine except for being in jail. He had been charged with reckless driving, under the influence, and no driver's license. They made him stay in jail until his court day.

Tammy, not having transportation, moved in with us after the accident.. She was relieved that Tony wasn't hurt, but mad at him for driving in the first place and drunk on top of that. She was upset that she had to move in with us and give up the nursery she had decorated for Joseph, yet she stayed as calm as she could for the remainder of her pregnancy for the baby's sake.

We all were worried this would start her labor. But she flowed through it all, like a well. Her goal then was to get him out of jail before the delivery. With work and the pressure of that, she would have to tell you what was going through her mind. But her love for Tony didn't waver. Through it all, she stayed calm. It was just another situation we would work through, was her attitude.

His court date came and she was there. We all hoped the judge would give him parole, but he didn't. Tony was sentenced and sent to jail. The time he had to serve meant he wouldn't be at the hospital for the birth of their baby. Tammy planned her days after that with visitation day included. She never once spoke any negative. She seemed to accept it as part of God's plan. She was there like clockwork every day she could see him. There was no doubt her heart ached for Tony to be with her through the remainder of her pregnancy and delivery. But she pushed forward with a smile and a positive attitude.

Our heart ached for her. We tried very hard to take as much work off her as possible. Except for her room, she had no chores. We hated that Tony was in jail, but we were happy that Tammy and the baby would be living with us. It broke her heart to have to share her room with the baby. Most of her plans for the nursery didn't happen. But she soon stopped crying and accepted what had happened. The miracle she carried inside reminded her daily that it was only material things. She reminded us that in time he would have his own room, his daddy would be home, and they would be in their own place again.

She used one of our vehicles as transportation until she could get one of her own. We worked on keeping her mind on the baby and happy thoughts. We asked about Tony each time she came home from a visit, and we allowed her to share what she felt like sharing. We didn't make any negative comments about the situation out of fear we would upset her.

March 13th,1989, Dr. Shannon talked like a c-section might be necessary. She was overdue, according to them, and not dilated or effaced. The baby's heartbeat was fluttering and weak. She was placed on a monitor twice a week after that, to keep check on his NST tests. Why they didn't admit her I don't know.

Then March 23rd arrived and she was in labor. Tammy said she felt funny and was shaking like a diabetic does. Sharp pains had begun. But instead of the doctors admitting her, he suggested she walk. She walked the hospital for several hours, but when nothing happened they discharged her. They suggested she stay close to the hospital.

Tammy, Penny and I went to the shopping center across from the hospital and walked all afternoon. When Tammy Joiner, Tony's sister, got off work, she joined us.

Later that evening around 6 p.m., we returned to the hospital. They suggested again that she walk the halls and hope her water would break.

A couple hours later, they suggested we go somewhere else for her to rest, but stay close to the hospital. So we went to her best friend Vanita's house. She only lived one mile from the hospital.

That night Tammy Joiner, Vanita and I took turns rubbing her back and legs. All night long she was in labor. We rubbed and timed every pain. She had deadly cramps in her back and legs. We told her to relax, but she couldn't. Her body was so stiff we didn't know what to do, so we kept rubbing and massaging all night long.

By morning, March 24th we were back at the hospital. We walked the hall until about noon. She had dilated 4 ccs and 100% effaced. She passed a brown and yellow heavy discharge and her water bag had leaked. They said all she had was a little water and baby poop, which was dangerous for the baby. Her blood work came back. It showed low oxygen, so they assigned her a bed. They hooked her up on the b-scan. At this point, I didn't think they thought Tammy or this baby would live.

I reached for the phone as soon as they left the room and asked Tammy Joiner to come in and sit with her. After I explained to her what the doctor said, I asked her to stay with Tammy. I wanted to call Aunt Sylvia, Uncle Early, and my work. I knew we needed a miracle, a favor from God, or something. Fear had set in. The thoughts of losing Tammy and this baby sickened my stomach. With my big mouth I stared them all in the face and threatened a lawsuit. Tears poured as I left her room to make the calls and ask for a prayer-chain. I gave them her name and phone number and asked for a miracle for the both of them.

Around 1 p.m. she was given oxygen and fluid was pumped in her to clean out the uterus. I couldn't believe they were allowing her to suffer like that. With each scream I became more afraid.

Around 2 p.m. Tammy received a phone call. He introduced himself as Rev. Bobby Ray of The Assembly of Faith, World Outreach Center, in Gastonia, N. C. This strange voice on the other end of her phone said, "God led me to call you and tell you, you will give birth to this baby. He will live a healthy life. You will live to raise him yourself." As he spoke, he revealed truths about Tammy that only Tammy would have known. Her hopes and faith in God showed in her face and eyes. He asked if he could pray, and Tammy agreed. Then suddenly the pastor's voice became loud and he shouted, "Oh My God! This child is born full of the Holy Spirit. His presence alone will bring glory to Almighty God." Then he went to speaking in a language unknown to Tammy. When he finished, he ended his conversation with these words, "Blessed is the woman who gives birth to this child. Cursed is any person who does harm to him, for he is surely a gift from God Himself, for this generation."

Around 3 p.m. hard labor pains began, and the medication they had given her had worn off.

4 p. m. The hard pushing began and I remembered the second dream. In all the confusion I hadn't even thought about that second dream until then. So I prayed for God to spare her a difficult deliver. But Aunt Sylvia was right, God had decided in the dream and her delivery was as painful as the dream. The only difference was that she was experiencing it, while I watched, as Gabriel had watched me. Why? We didn't know.

By 4:30 p.m. they discovered the baby was lying on its side with his head flopped over. Tammy and the baby had the doctors' and nurses' full attention by then. They went to work on turning him. By this time Tammy was listed as critical. Her heart rate was 210 and her blood pressure very high. Tammy hung onto every ounce of hope and faith she had.

Yet was it enough? Would God take her this far and then just let her die? Were the prayers of her mom's coworkers and church friends enough? Was this baby going to be born without a mom to raise him? Would the answer come in time to save both baby and mom? Were the words from Rev. Bobby Ray correct? At 7:30 p.m., after five hours or more of pushing and turning, the doctor said the baby was turned. Let's get him out of there, one of them said.

With a suction cup and Tammy pushing, they literally pulled that baby out. He was out and into the world, but no movement or breath yet. I watched as Tammy strained to see if he was breathing. She kept repeating, "He's not breathing. He's not breathing." One team proceeded to help Tammy while the other team took the baby and pumped his lungs out.

Then he cried. He caught his breath or the life of God and let out such a scream, we all laughed. Tammy flopped back onto the bed with a sign of relief. She could finally catch her breath and relax. His cry was music to our ears. The sweetest sound any of us had ever heard.

A young twenty-two year old woman who was sterile had a baby, with blond hair, blue eyes, web feet, and long fingers like his physical daddy. His color was as rosy as a pink rose. The nurses and doctor continued to work on him as

we watched.

It wasn't long before they had him weighed in at 7 pounds and three ounces. He was twenty-one inches long. His head measured at thirteen and half inches with a chest that measured thirteen and one forth inches. The doctor announced he was a healthy little boy.

At that time, the nurse proceeded to clean him up and placed his little blue cap on his head. Then she handed him to Tammy to hold. The smile on her face revealed all the pain was worth it. I watched, as they starred at each other, sharing one big smile from each of them together. His face was as if he was saying, "Hi Mom." Silence filled the room except what came from the doctors and nurses and

out in the hall.

"Look, mama. Look at his big smile," Tammy said as she fondled his fingers. How long she held him, I didn't time it, but before she handed him to me she had unwrapped him and examined his feet and every inch of his body. Then she handed him to me.

"Proud grandmother", all the staff said. I caught myself doing what Tammy had done earlier, smiling and noticing his starry eyes full of light. How long I stared? I don't have a clue.

The nurses and doctor left the three of us alone, while the cleaning staff cleaned the room and removed all the stuff. All we could talk about was the baby. Tammy didn't mention Tony but I knew how she felt. I remembered my own feelings when she was born and her daddy was in Germany serving his country. I didn't have to ask her, I knew how she felt.

The nurse returned a little later and asked if we wanted the family to see the baby before she took him down to the nursery. Suddenly both of us remembered and said at the same time, "Family." In a hurry then, I said yes, and ran to the door to make the announcement.

Tammy Joiner said, "I knew by your smile he was here." They all rushed in as soon as I said they could see him. Sam beat them all to the room and was the first one to hold him. Joseph looked up at Papa and smiled. We all witnessed Sam's heart melt right before our eyes.

Cameras went to flashing, the movie camera was filming, and every expression and comment was recorded. Everyone wanted to know why they hadn't given Tammy a c-section. But the only answer we had was, they said they waited too long and it was too dangerous. Tammy shared every detail of her ordeal. She announced after all the glorious details that she would never have another baby there.

Soon the nurse returned and took Joseph, and said we could see him later. For now he needed to go to the nursery, and Tammy needed to go to her room and rest.

Every blood vessel in Tammy's face had busted, which told the story of her painful labor and delivery. She had surely suffered a near death experience and fought hard to bring this baby into the world. Her blood pressure was still a little high, but other than that she was fine. We all said we had people to call anyway and were hungry as we gathered our things. As we proceeded to leave the room I saw Tammy lay her head back on the pillow and relax for the first time in two days. She asked Tammy Joiner to call Tony.

One nurse had taken the baby, and another had proceeded to get Tammy ready to be transported to her room. We all departed and went our separate ways to make our calls and eat, but none of us were leaving the hospital.

An hour or so later, Tammy was settled in her new room and everyone left the hospital. They had already told her she wouldn't get to see the baby any more that night; his nurse would care him for. We all hoped she would sleep well all night.

The next morning was Saturday, and such a beautiful day at that. Penny and I were at the hospital by eight. Tammy was sitting up in her bed with the baby in her arms. When she looked up at me, her face seemed worried. She said, "Mama, he won't take the bottle, and I don't have any breast milk. What are we going to do?"

I smiled and asked her to give him to me. I worked with him, sticking the nipple in his mouth and squeezing the milk in. Then I rubbed the nipple around his lips and showed her how to do it. We took turns and worked with him. He licked his lips like the milk was good but he was too lazy to nurse. We laughed at him and kept working with him.

Finally I suggested we pray over him and give him back to God. Tammy looked at me like she didn't have a clue of what I had said. I explained it to her, and she agreed. I prayed, and she repeated it as she held him up from her chest like a love offering. We thanked God for this blessing. We asked him to protect him and keep him safe. We asked God to get all of the glory in his conception, birth, and life on earth. We asked him to forgive us for our doubts and disbelief. As we prayed the prayer of thanksgiving and asked for guidance, last, but not least, we asked that he would take his bottle also. Both of us let out loud laughs as we said amen.

Between the two of us, after another hour or so, he took his bottle. That boy ate like he hadn't eaten in a month. Soon he was finished. In a few minutes we began to smell the worst smell. Tammy peeped in his diaper and announced it was him. He smelt rotten. I told her I was getting the doctor or nurse, to see why his poop smelled so rotten. The doctor was at the desk and came back with me. He smiled and announced that he was getting all of his minerals and vitamins out of his food. It was the right color, brown. He was just fine. Then he left the room. We had a big laugh over that, too. So far we found joy in everything he did.

Soon he was fast asleep on the foot of Tammy's bed. We just watched him breathe as he slept. The nurse broke the silence when she came in and asked what his name would be. I immediately announced, "Joseph."

But Tammy spoke up quickly to let me know we needed to talk about that. I immediately jumped to God's defense and said, "That's the name the Archangel said." The nurse left us alone to discuss it when she saw Tammy's expression and my reaction to that announcement.

Tammy slowly said, "Mama, I understand that. The name we decided on means the same thing." She saw I had gotten upset and continued. "Mama, his name will be Michael Lee Johns. Michael is the English version of Joseph."

"But Gabriel said to call him Joseph, not Michael," I added.

Tammy messed with her covers as she reached to touch Michael's feet and continued, "Mama, I want his name to be Michael. I don't think God will mind if I name my son that name. Besides, it means the same." Then she paused as I sat down on the bed and took his finger. Silence filled the room for a few seconds as we both pondered over the name change. We had called him Joseph for eight months and she hadn't said a word about changing it. Now this morning

I was faced with this surprise.

"Who thought of that, Tony?" I asked in an angry tone.

But she immediately jumped to his defense as forcefully as I had earlier. "Mama, you pray about it. We will wait until we all agree before I fill out his birth certificate. It's not Tony, but me. I looked it up and it means the same. Like Jesus was called Joshua in some places, but it meant the same thing." She continued her argument until I gave in. Soon thereafter the nurse returned with the papers again and asked if we were ready. I got up off the bed as she said, "Yes. We are ready. His name is Michael Lee Johns."

I was worried about this name change but said nothing more. I figured I would study and see what God had to say about it. God reminded me that He had only one name, Creator, Yahweh. Yet he had many titles. Jesus had only one name, Yeshua, and Yeshua was the name Gabriel spoke to Mary; the Son of the most High God-Elohim. After that I received peace and let it go.

Uncle Early said this baby was a sign for his generation. He would usher in the Supernatural. That the world events would bring change in his generation, change like the world has never seen before.

One dream remained to come to pass out of three. We had fifteen months before we would see that fulfillment. I decided to keep the third dream a secret except for a small handful of people I had entrusted with it.

Now, I will list just a few world events that Google search provided that took place in 1988. The same year the archangel Gabriel announced the birth of Michael.

1988: Howard Dicus: As superpower relations got warmer, there was a cooling for world hotspots. Ceasefires, troop pullouts and other peace moves took place in Afghanistan, Cambodia, Nicaragua and Angola. Near the year's end, PLO leader Yasser Arafat renounced terrorism.

1988: The US answered by opening direct talks with the PLO for the first time ever. A ceasefire interrupted the eight-year Iran-Iraq war. The US ship sent the guard tankers through the war zone, were able to head home. Before peace came, American guns were more than once turned on Iranian attackers, and once in the middle of a naval engagement with Iran, the US shot down an Iranian airliner, killing all 290 aboard. Admiral William Crowe, Chairman of the Joint Chiefs of Staff.

1988: Iran said America would pay, but denied involvement when late in the year, a Pan Am flight from Frankfurt and London apparently exploded over Scotland. All on board were killed, as were many on the ground when wreckage rained on a Scottish town like liquid fire. To use the words of witness, Mike Carnahan.

1988: Mike Carnahan: "The time that it went up, there was a terrible explosion and the whole sky lit up and it was virtually raining fire. It was just like liquid fire."

1988: Well-known Washington figures were convicted of crimes in 1988. They included former Reagan aides Michael Deaver and Lyn Nofziger, each found guilty of influence peddling. John Poindexter and his deputy were indicted in the Iran Contra affair. Oliver North threatened to put VIP's on the stand if the case ever came to trial.

1988: Longest Undersea Tunnel Opens. A railroad tunnel opened between Aomori on the Honshu Island and Hakidate in Hokkaido, Japan . The tunnel, called "Seikan," was 33.44 miles long and was as deep as 787 feet below water at one point.

Because pre-millennial time indicators have flopped, Israel in 1948 (The "last generation" seeing Jesus come in '88, with an '81 rapture), and Jerusalem in 1967, Bible Prophecy teachers are relaying more and more upon the "Thousand year model" of interpretation. If this model is to be taken in such a manner, then the reverse would be true as well, and the thousand-year reign of Christ would extend for the duration of one day. A generation has passed (40 years, Heb.3:9,10) since 1948, and Jesus did not come. {The False Prophets proven wrong to whole world}

What does the Word say about Endtime, and what proof do we have based on the word of God that we are living in resurrection and restoration times? Listed below are a few of John Owens' research notes, a Puritan. Thanks to Google search engines.

The last days were the last days of the Old Covenant system, which revolved around the temple. (Acts 2:16-21, Heb.1:2) The New Covenant temple of which revolved around the temple. (Acts 2:16-21, Heb.1:2) {Every Prophecy must line up with the word of God to be truth.}

The body of Christ is clearly revealed after the Old temple is destroyed. (Heb.9:8) This New temple is the temple/tabernacle (Rev.21:3) of God described as a *"New Heaven and a New Earth"* (Rv.21:1), a *New Jerusalem* (Rev.21:2, Gal.4:26-New Covenant, Hb.12:22) and as a *BRIDE* (Rev.21:2, Rom.7:4, 2 Cor.11:2). The bride of Christ, which is His *body/temple/tabernacle*. (Col.1:24) God's covenant people are the dwelling place of God from *Heaven* joined with men on the *Earth*. This is His will being done on *Earth* as it is in *Heaven*. (Mt.6:10)

The Puritan theologian John Owen comes to this conclusion concerning the references in 2 Pet.3:7,10,12,and 13, to the *Old*, verses the *New Heavens and*

Earth. He makes the connection with the Old Testament's use of the terms in relationship to a covenant people. "And I have put my words in thy mouth, and I have covered thee in the shadow of mine hand, that I may plant the *HEAVENS*, and lay the foundations of the *EARTH*, and say unto Zion, Thou art *MY PEOPLE*." (Is.51:16)

Moses addresses this Covenant people in this same way when he states, "Give ear, O ye *HEAVE[1]NS*, and I will speak; and hear, O *EARTH*, the words of my mouth." (Deut.32:1) Isaiah does the same again when he says, "Hear, O *HEAVEN[1]S*, and give ear, O *EARTH*…" (Isaiah 1:2) This New Covenant has no end, it is everlasting. (Heb.13:20) It is entirely impossible to force a last days in the phrase "Ever*lasting* Covenant."

There is no end to the physical earth, only an end to a vanishing Old Covenant system in the first century. (Heb.8:13) An end to the Old Covenant Age.

Now, on a more personal note: In 1988 Carolyn Smith Phillips wrote her first book, A DADDY, BUT NO MAMA. Written through the eyes of a child.

Now take a look at some of the world events in 1989:

1989 Berlin Wall Comes Down On October 18, the regime of Erich Hoenecker, the Communist leader of East Germany, fell. It succumbed to increasing riots, as well as a flood of East Germans leaving via the open borders of Hungary . On November 10, the new government announced the end of all travel restrictions, and soon thousands of Berliners took part in taking down the Berlin Wall that had divided the city for 27 years.

In 1988 The Archangel Gabriel announced Michael's birth in three separate dreams to his grandmother.

All of the above had to come to pass according to Uncle Early and Aunt Sylvia, who stated that spiritually it meant that the wall of ignorance had come down and the minds that separated us from God were falling. That the teaching that God is far away will fall and people will realize that the Holy Spirit is God. That God is three parts just like he created male and female. And the three parts must now come forth as one new man, the God Man, God Woman. That Father God, Mother God and Son God are in reality One Creator God. They said the Bible teaches us, and we must receive by revelation, that we are three parts also, spirit, soul and body that are becoming one new man/woman. That more people would realize that the Holy Spirit is within all that believes. The cross restored our life resurrection and our total restoration and brought the kingdom of God alive within us that hear what the Spirit has to say. We shall live to experience this promise and experience the earth in all of God's Glory.

"Let us make man in *our* image and *our* likeness. Let us make male and female alike in *our* likeness and *our* image." We are three parts revealed by God after the cross. We are spirit, soul and body.

When Michael was born, Uncle Early said it was time for the spirit of ignorance to leave the churches and preachers to start teaching truth. He said world preachers living behind a mask of darkness/ignorance leading God's children into further darkness would be revealed and exposed. And the people sitting in the pews are the ones God will use, for they are hungry for truth. That a new teaching would begin: That God wasn't up there somewhere, when in truth, God was and is within each of us. That God took the dust of the earth and made man, and then God breathed into man/woman and made them a living soul. He said that some need to wake up. Some need to grow up. That's why Christ came and did away with the wall of ignorance that separated us from God. The separation was only in the mind, for when the breath of God leaves a body, that body is dead.

1989 Earthquake Hits San Francisco An earthquake measuring 6.9 on the Richter scale hit the San Francisco area. The quake killed 57 people but caused nearly $10 billion in damages.

March 24th 1989 Michael Lee Johns was born to Tammy Carol and Tony Johns. The first two dreams had come to pass.

Uncle Early again stated the earthquakes were a spiritual sign as well. He said, God was gonna shake the ignorance out of us all. He said there would be more and stronger earthquakes upon the earth all over the earth, and we would see and hear about them more in the next twenty years. And God would awaken scientists to realize that truth would prove God's word to be truth.

1989 The First Liver Transplant The first liver transplant, using a live donor, took place at the Chicago Medical Center. (Our family had this experience first hand when Penny's husband Chris Lacks had a liver transplant at UVA and he passed May 2008, just one month before Michael passed.)

Also in 1989: The author, Carolyn S. Phillips, published her first book, A DADDY BUT NO MAMA, She was listed in various newspapers around the country and made appearances on radio and T.V. talk shows in the Florida area. She was a regular guest on one of Jacksonville's radio talk shows for a year.

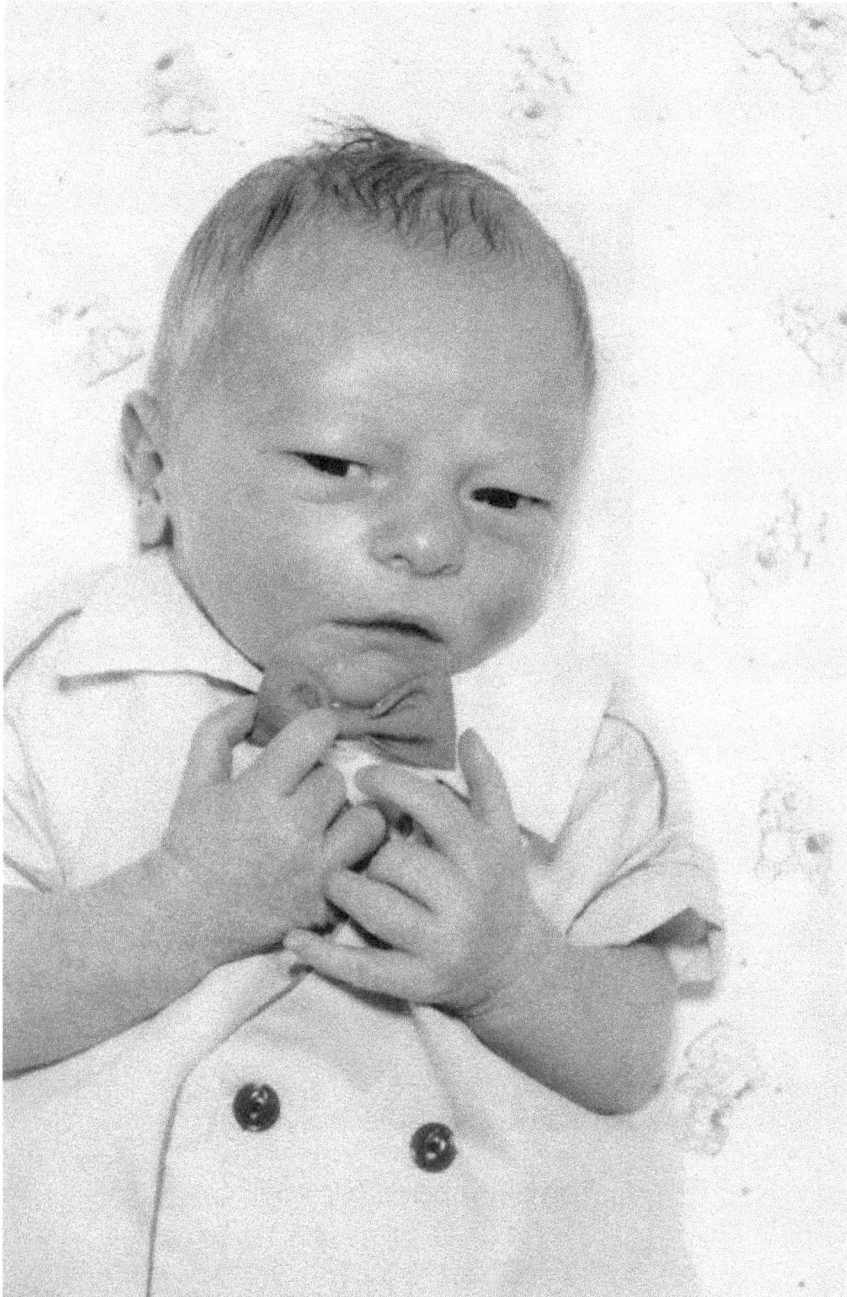

Michael Lee Johns
Born: March 24th 1989

Tony, Michael, Tammy

CHAPTER SIX

AN ORDINARY BABY OR NOT

CHAPTER SIX

AN ORDINARY BABY OR NOT

Michael had been conceived and born on this earth, as the first two dreams had showed us. Now we waited the next fifteen months for the third dream to manifest itself. On March 27th, 1989, Michael was circumcised and Tammy was discharged. Our first stop was at Vanita's so her mother who had been ill could see him. From there we went to my office. I played the proud grandmother's role. Tammy enjoyed showing him off. Everyone there was so excited. They had to touch him to make sure he was real. They called him 'the miracle baby'. From there we stopped by the grocery store to buy formula. The last stop was 4509 Cedar Point Road, home as we knew it. Tammy got him settled in his bed while I cleaned a little. We both knew the house would be full of people soon. Sure enough, La Gina, Cheryl, Uncle Early, Aunt Sylvia, Warren and Pat showed up one behind the other within the first hour. To the world Michael might have been just an ordinary baby. But to those who knew the story of his conception and birth, he was anything but ordinary.

On April 1st she took him to visit his daddy for the first time. The following months Tammy carried him with her everywhere, even to work with her on the bus. Tony's family had been very supportive through it all. She visited them often. She kept them posted on Tony and Michael's progress. Michael cooed and played possum with a smile as if he knew what he was doing. Tony got a kick out that. With each visit from his wife and son, he became more determined to stay on good behavior for early release. He regretted not being there for Tammy and promised to make it up to her and Michael.

I had announced his birth and told his story on my weekly radio talk show there in Jacksonville. I even shared it on the television talk shows I had been invited to. Phone calls came in often to see how he was doing. Newspapers picked up the story and did several interviews. His big ears made the joke line a few times.

Our church became very interested in his progress and was also supportive. But soon we learned he wasn't any different from any other child. He cried when he was hungry and wet. Slept a lot, laughed a lot, flipped over on his side when he wanted to and sucked his fist a lot. His Uncle Johnny and Aunt Sharlene Wallace gave him three years of clothes and different baby items. What a blessing they were! Michael's birth had helped heal their hearts. They had lost their baby boy about the time Tammy announced she was pregnant.

As time passed, changes also continued to unfold. Most of them weren't easy to accept. But Michael's presence just seemed to work them all too good. We lived through each one believing they were a stepping-stone to fulfilling the third dream.

Tony was out of jail and we knew it wouldn't be long before they would move to their own place. We dreaded to even think of that day. But it came and they moved and we survived that ordeal as well, after many tears. We didn't see Michael every day after that, and oh, how he was missed. Our hearts ached to be in his presence. But Tammy and Tony both soon realized that Michael was more to us than just any ordinary baby and they began coming over more. We were always so thankful to them for that and helped them in any way we could to make their life richer. I don't believe there was anything they asked that Sam or I or both of us didn't fulfill for them. Our love for money, wealth and fame had melted. God and family had become the most important focus in our lives. We wanted to show our appreciation and love and help them. We didn't want them to want for anything. If Jay, Wendy, Nell or Penny were ever envious of them and the help we provided, they never showed it. They were just as pleased to help as we were.

Uncle Early saw him as a generational sign to wake up sleeping souls, he called it. That set him and Aunt Sylvia on fire to preach even more than before. They were traveling from meeting to meeting all over the country. Another change we didn't like, because we didn't see them every day any more, but soon after we realized we needed their strength and guidance and started attending some of their out of town meetings. As Sam put it, we just couldn't stay away from them and that good food.

Jay and Wendy had graduated from high school. Wendy was working at my office in filing. Jay had moved back to Virginia and was working at Hardies with a close friend of mine while he waited for Presto to call him.

June 1989 came and we went to the reunion. Michael met his Papa Creasy and other family members for the first time. I watched Aunt Ellen as she held him and studied him in all smiles as though she was holding her first great-grand baby. Michael became more spoiled as he was shown off to family and friends while in Virginia. But he stayed as sweet and humble as he was before the extra spoiling.

Michael's first Christmas came in 1989, and we decided to spend it in Jacksonville so he would enjoy both his mama's and dad's family. We put Wendy and Nell on the bus and sent them to their grandmother's in Virginia, where they wanted to be for Christmas. Shirley and a friend decided to come down and spend Christmas with us. She said she had never missed a Christmas with me and was too old to start now. Tammy and Tony also decided to start a new tradition and stayed at our house Christmas Eve so we would see Michael get Santa and open gifts.

By the time we realized Jacksonville was receiving the worst snow and ice storm in over a hundred years, my sister Shirley and her friend were already on their way. They slipped from side to side and almost wrecked several times. While they battled the storm making history, I tried not to worry and cooked to help me stay in faith that all would be well with them and us. By the time they walked in the door I had enough food cooked to feed an army. Everyone laughed about all the food, but the laughter stopped when the power went off.

I saw Shirley's face as they walked in the house around midnight, frightened as if she had seen a ghost or an angel. They were so tired and yet so glad to be there in the warm presence of family. Soon they had settled in and we dug into the stew and ham with pie for dessert as we talked, laughed and waited for Tony to get there. Constantly we were sending up prayers as we watched Tammy going to the window looking out for him.

Tony had gotten caught in the storm at his grandparents. The bridges had closed and we didn't know how he would get home that night. As we pondered over that and the storm and how bad it was really getting, fear was trying it best to mess up our faith. When Tony called and said he would be there if he had to walk, fear felt stronger in the house. The storm was so boisterous we feared for his life if he tried to walk. We all heard Tammy crying as she begged him to stay at his grandparents and come Christmas Day. But as usual Tony won out and said he would be there for his son's Christmas or die trying, and hung up.

Around three o'clock he walked in the side door almost frozen to death, with the biggest smile across his face. Tammy ran and hugged him while unwrapping him and fussing at him for walking home in that terrible storm. But when he walked in that door, the rest of us were so happy he was there all we could do was laugh at them.

 He said, "Where's my boy?" as he walked over to me and picked him up.

Tammy calmed down but hung onto him like glue. Her face had showed us she had almost fainted when he walked in so cold and covered in so much snow. She was also pleased he was alive and not missing Michael's first Christmas. With Tony, Shirley and the rest of the family and Michael there, and plenty of food, we all settled in and relaxed.

When the power came back on the news said we had the worst ice storm Jacksonville had ever seem. Bridges and roads were closed all over the state. Power went on and off for several hours that Christmas Eve before it finally went out until morning. That meant no furnace, so we heated with the fireplace in the living room. We had pulled all blankets and pillows and anything else that would make the floor more comfortable for everyone. We had wall to wall people in that huge living room that looked so small. Everyone stepping over blankets and stuff and people, but we seemed to have found joy in all of it.

Thank God I had cooked all that food. We had plenty of bread, ham, and turkey for sandwiches. Beans and stew we put in an iron skillet and heated in the fireplace. Potato salad and other veggies, we could eat cold if necessary. Cakes, pies and cookies as desserts we could grab and run to the fireplace and eat. It brought back so many memories of my childhood Christmases at Aunt Ellen's with the entire Smith family around her table, laughing and enjoying fellowship and food.

Tony kept the fireplace roaring. He was such a blessing and had such a good and appreciative attitude. It was all we had to heat by, and with that large living room, dining room and kitchen opened it was a lot to heat. Tony carried in so much wood and kept us all warm, grabbing a piece of cake, or a cookie or something, he would run back out to get more.

To top it all off, Sam had strep throat and ran a fever. It was the first time he had been sick since we married, and he was really sick. We stayed away from him as much as possible and totally off the sofa where he lay.

With all that, we still had Santa to put together and gifts to go under the tree that Christmas Eve. Santa had brought Michael a wagon and tricycle, which with Sam sick Shirley's friend had put together. It didn't take her long to see that all of our nerves were shot and any little thing would drive us from laughter to tears. She was a stranger when she got there, but oh, the blessing she was. By the time Christmas was over and they were headed back to Danville, Virginia, she had become a dear friend to us all.

With nerves on edge and yet so thankful to be together, we made a special effect to stay in good moods. But with Tony around that wasn't hard at all. He in his funny, joking way, made all it seem like a blessing. He said God wanted us all to smell each other's feet. That's why we had to camp out so close. That God wanted us to know that it didn't matter how large a house was, we only needed room for another pair of stinking feet, as he pushed Shirley over to sit beside her and hug her. Everyone knew he was making jokes about him and Michael's feet stinking so badly. Shirley laughed until she cried at his jokes. He said Ma Carolyn prayed for an old fashioned Virginia Christmas in Jacksonville, and that's what we got. Everyone laughed and answered with a smart response of their own, but all agreed for me to stop praying for an old-fashioned Christmas.

The cutest one of all was when Sam rose up off the sofa bed where he had appeared to be at death's door and said, "That old-fashioned Christmas she prayed for should have included electricity, instead of one like the good ole days when our great-grandparents were on the earth." He didn't stop to take a breath in between words, but his head was slowly falling to the pillow as he fell backwards and took a breath. We knew it took all his energy to get his say-so in. His scratchy voice, so low after listening to his loud authoritative one, cracked everyone up. Laughter and more laughter filled the room until we were all crying and trying to stop laughing. But Sam never cut a smile. He was serious about that electricity business.

Well, as each day passed it got easier and easier. The electricity had come back on and everyone was glad to get a shower and sleep in a bed. We had gotten through the Jacksonville ole fashioned white Christmas and life went on to unfold.

Soon we would be celebrating Michael's first birthday, March 24th 1990. Questions about him had risen as the doctors had learned what they shared with us about his physical and mental state. We had learned on Michael's September doctor's visit that he was two to three months ahead of other infants in intelligence. That confirmed what we had witnessed all along the way about his fast learning and his how to do whatever he wanted. He could study a table or pool ball and figure out how to get it. They said he was gifted with his hands and motor skills.

We were even asked if we thought he was the Christ in the flesh. We all laughed at that one. We figured they were testing our mental intelligence as well. We did tell them that the angel that announced his birth was the same angel that announced John the Baptist and Jesus's birth.

Uncle Early wanted to answer that one and said Michael was a living manifestation as to what the living word in the flesh meant. That he was a sign for his generation to wake up and realize the power of God's presence. He was also aware to those that continued to reject truth and recognize God's presence. He continued and said for us to draw near unto God and realize that God is all authority in heaven and earth, and he has given all that authority to Christ. And now Christ was ready with that authority to reveal it in us, those that believe it.

He said we would witness in the coming years where preachers will preach and teachers will teach that God is found in intimacy. An intimate relationship energized in such a way that it would be closer than a husband and wife's relationship, and far better than any sexual pleasure. That God was revealing himself in a special way again to many around the world, and the whole world would know about it. It wouldn't be isolated to a few or one small town or small country, but for all. All over the world people would see the manifestation of God in ordinary people, more so than in the preachers, special manifestations in and to ordinary people.

That Christ working with the Holy Spirit was gonna tear down man's old traditions, man-made gods, and all those old rules. The old law was finished and we were coming out of it to live in the new law of love. Some of us would wake up and realize we were the temple of God and what that meant. That it was after Moses committed murder that he saw God in a special way. That it was after Jesus was murdered that souls woke up and saw signs, wonders, and miracles performed by people. He said it was after Saul abused Christians and killed them that he saw Christ in full light resurrected and restored, and it was time for his children of light to resurrect and be restored and seen by those God has chosen.

That since Jesus's death, burial and resurrection we have been in conception in the tomb of darkness, growing to a baby stage so we would be strong and come forth. Now it was time to come forth, wake up and learn to feed ourselves and grow up.

That while Peter was in Jesus's presence, he could walk on water. But soon thereafter he denied even knowing him. He had to learn to be led by the Holy Spirit. Even his shadow healed people as he walked down the streets. That Paul saw and experienced a vision that changed his life, and the time had come for many Peters and Pauls to come forth. That Michael was a sign that the end of the old age had come, not the end of the world, but the end of the old way of life. Uncle Early was bold when he said our prayer should be that we may know HIM and the power of HIS resurrection and total restoration. He said when we stay focused on that prayer, then we would see Christ manifested on this earth in a glorious way, not in that gloom and doom way. He said all that was fear-based to keep people in ignorance so they could sell books and tapes. That was a lot of knowledge back then. I had to put most of it on the shelf and wait for understanding, as he had advised us to do.

Time had continued to move, and with each day I knew the day would come to fulfill the last dream of our move to Virginia. Halloween was here and Tammy had dressed Michael as a mouse since he loved Mickey Mouse dolls. That's when he was given the Georgia Bull Dog doll and the Jacksonville Jaguar doll. It was soon after that we learned he liked the Bull Dogs better, like his daddy. Tony loved that since his daddy's people were from Georgia. He could ride his mama's family with jokes forever after that. He called Michael a true rebel.

Michael's Papa Sammy had him driving a battery-operated jeep while he was crawling on his knees, to teach him how to drive before he was a year old. We all enjoyed watching that and made jokes that we couldn't get him to bow, but Michael did. He also had Michael up on the pool table and shooting pool before his first birthday and riding a power-operated hobbyhorse that he learned how to not fall off. He had turned his loud and arrogant Papa Sammy into a bowl of cherries or candy in his hands. Michael was the star of our hearts and our full attention. He had turned us all back into little kids and had blessed us all with the gift of joy again.

Then January 1990 came. Michael was ten months old when he climbed up on my coffee table on his own in his cowboy boots and cowboy outfit. Holster on his waist and two guns in his hands, shooting at us, "Bang, bang," as he shot us with that big smile stretched out over his face. Immediately I remembered the first sign in the third dream. I ran to tell the family we would be moving in five months back to Virginia. Nell and Penny were the only ones excited at that time to hear the news. It made all the others sad, and they tried to talk me out of it. But I knew God was going to do what he said and I had to obey or be miserable the rest of my life. I knew I couldn't change God's mind. He had Michael in his sights and had a plan for him on earth, and he would carry it out, with us or not. They knew it too, but were so happy that they feared it would go back to the old way. They had settled in and made Jacksonville home since Michael was born. We knew it also meant Michael would be leaving Aunt Sylvia and Uncle Early and his daddy's family behind. All of us were sad about that and wondered why God wanted Michael to live and grow up in Virginia rather than Jacksonville. But we all knew God had answered and brought to pass the first two dreams his way, so we waited for the second sign. Some people prayed that God would change his mind and the second sign wouldn't come.

March 24th 1990, Michael's first birthday at his Nana Carolyn's with all family members that lived in Jacksonville attending. Enough presents for three to five babies, yet he enjoyed the birthday paper more than any of it. Michael enjoyed his first birthday cake, with it all over his hands and face. He also enjoyed rubbing the icing in his hair, while we all took pictures and laughed. He was the life of the party that day. The birthday party ended when the question arose when we would we be moving back to Virginia, and I answered, when God spoke.

His first Easter, he was a natural outside hunting for eggs. We had learned early on that it didn't take but once and he knew how to and wanted to do it himself.

It was June and Michael was fifteen months old. School was out and plans were made for the trip to Virginia. The Smith reunion and summer break in Virginia were two yearly goals everyone looked forward to for six years.

This reunion gave the second sign of the third dream. We had eaten and were just sitting around shooting the breeze, when a cousin's wife mentioned that I should go and apply at the unemployment office and get my old job back. They were begging for experienced help. My heart leaped and I knew immediately it was God who had spoken through her. I looked up at her and said thank you. I will. Some made jokes and said that I was so conceited to think I was that good, that they actually would call me in Jacksonville. I laughed it off, for my family had always picked on me, but only a few knew about my dreams, visions, and visitations with angels and Jesus. But Monday morning I did apply for my old job.

Middle of June, Faye called me at work in Jacksonville and asked if I could come up for a physical that Thursday. Since it was a Monday, she said, that meant I would have to leave on Wednesday. If I could go and pass the physical, then I had my old job back and would start July 1st. I gave her a happy yes. The second sign of the third dream was about to be fulfilled.

I came up and passed with flying colors, had the interview and by the next day was headed back to Jacksonville to give my notice. I called ahead of time and told Sam and Tammy to start packing.

Between God, family and friends, God had worked out every detail and provided an army of helpers. My house in Virginia was under lease. Therefore Penny, Michael and I would move in with Jay for a few months. Tammy and Tony would follow a week later with one U-haul. I had found them a mobile home for rent with electric on and ready for their arrival. Aunt Sylvia and Uncle Early would help Sam with the last load when he was ready to leave a few months later. We had already liquidated some real estate in the past fifteen months. But we still had about ten properties left, plus his T.V. business. Even though we came in stages, the way it all flowed and blended so beautifully, it amazed us beyond words. We just knew unless God gave me more dreams and visions, we wouldn't have a clue as to God's plan or purpose for the remainder of this boy wonder, Michael, who had entered our hearts and lives these past fifteen months.

I could go on and brag as any grandmother loves to do about their grandchild, but instead, I want others to tell you about Michael. Through the eyes of his mother, sister, uncle, aunt, and a few friends, you will see that like God says, children are truly a gift from God. You see, Michael was shot and killed June 21st, 2008, in his own home. That's another story that I will share with you at a later date.

Michael was just one of many of our children in this country that didn't live to finish out his goals on earth. You or someone you know might have also lost a child, grandchild, brother, sister, nephew, niece or friend whose life was cut short. Leaving many unanswered questions along with that empty place at your table. I hope something in this book will help your heart to heal. Help you find some of your answers. I hope you know that they are still with us.

But for now, I hope you enjoy the few little stories that follow, written in their own words about Michael. And I also hope you watch for the second book published, MICHAEL, SUICIDE OR MURDER, when we will share the rest of the story.

CHAPTER SEVEN

MICHAEL THROUGH THE EYES OF HIS MOM

CHAPTER SEVEN

MICHAEL THROUGH THE EYES OF HIS MOM

Michael was my first miracle child. Several doctors told me that I couldn't have children because I didn't ovulate properly. I tried for several years to become pregnant, yet nothing seemed to work. At the very moment that I thought I had accepted the fact that I wouldn't have any children, I became pregnant with my first miracle. It was at this point that I started to believe, that with God, I could overcome what the doctors had told me. My dream was to always have a boy and a girl. I knew from the beginning of the pregnancy that I was having a boy, even though I didn't have a sonogram that confirmed my belief because they didn't do them at that time. That didn't matter. I prepared for a boy for my entire pregnancy.

Michael was due the end of February. The doctors took me out of work at the end of January. Because I drove a school bus and the constant leaning and pulling was becoming stressful to the baby, they said. We lived in the rural area of Florida, but my mom worked in the city of Jacksonville. So every day after that, she would take me to a friend's house that was only five minutes from the hospital and only ten minutes from her job. I was 23 years old and needed a babysitter every day. February came and went and there still was no baby.

Around the second week of March I started telling the doctor that my water was leaking and the baby wasn't moving very much. The doctor believed that the baby was putting pressure on my bladder, causing me to urinate all of the time. He said the baby was getting ready for delivery and that's why he wasn't moving a lot.

I went to the doctor about a week before he was born. They couldn't find his heartbeat and there was no movement. The doctor told me to prepare for a stillborn child. I was upset, but I refused to think that God had given me the miracle of becoming pregnant and then taken the blessed child away from me.

My mom started a prayer chain with family members, friends and churches. All of these family members, friends and churches contacted their own families, friends and churches. Soon I had people all over the world praying for my baby and me.

It was later that day that a preacher from South Carolina called me on the phone to pray with me. He didn't know my family or me, but felt led by God to call me. We talked on the phone for a while and he asked me lots of questions about me, my life, my child and what the doctors had told me. Finally he asked if he could pray with me over the phone. At this point I was scared, upset and wanted to do anything that would save my baby. He prayed a very short prayer with me. He asked God to bring forth this miracle child and fulfill my dreams of being a mother. It was at this very moment that Michael leaped in my stomach like he was swimming in a swimming pool. He didn't slow down very much until the day before he was born after that.

On March 23, 1989, I was at my babysitter's house while mom was working. Around 11:00 am I called mom and told her that I felt funny. I couldn't explain how I felt, but just that I felt funny. Mom got off of work and we went home and prepared for Michael to come that night. The labor pains started but they weren't very hard. I took my shower, and then I got all of my things together for the hospital.

We arrived at the hospital around 8:00 pm that night. The doctor told me it was too early and to go back home. He said that if my water didn't break before morning, then to come to my regular appointment, at 9:00 am.

We stayed at my friend's house so we would be close to the hospital that night hoping that my water would break. It wasn't long before I started labor pains in my back. They got so tense that the pain would shoot down my legs. My mother, my friend Vanita, and my sister-in-law Tammy stayed up all night taking turns rubbing my back and legs.

The next morning I went to my regular doctor's appointment as I was asked to do. I remember standing in the hall having severe pains in my back and legs, and they wouldn't even give me a wheelchair to sit in. Mom and my sister-in-law asked for a place where I could sit down, but the nurse showed us no compassion. After several hours and my pains had increased, my sister-in-law finally threw a fit. She cussed out the nurse. We'd had enough of their attitude. At this point she was demanding for someone to come and check me over.

It must have worked, because they took me in the back room and told me to give them a urine sample. When I went to the bathroom I had very brown mucus looking discharge. When I showed it to the nurse, they started scrambling then. She went immediately and got the doctor to examine me. We knew from the look on their faces that something was wrong. After the doctor finished examining me, he said that I didn't have any water left in my sac and the baby was swallowing his own poop.

They immediately took me to a room and started fluids and preparing for this baby to come. My mom was videotaping the entire process. I was in so much pain at that point that I had started screaming. I had been in labor since about 11:00 am the previous day. One nurse came in and told me to stop screaming. She said that I knew how I got pregnant and that I should just be quiet. That other women were there and they weren't screaming.

Well, my mom went off. She told her to get out. Then she told the entire nursing staff that if that nurse came back into my room she was going to smack her. I stayed in pain most of that day.

Later another nurse came in and told me to start pushing with my contractions. Maybe the baby would come sooner. I kept pushing and suffering like she said, even though no one had examined me to see what was happening since earlier in the day when the doctor had examined me.

Then that afternoon the head nurse came in. She immediately wanted to know why I hadn't had that baby. She reached for the sheet and pulled the covers back. Then she covered me back and immediately took the nurse on duty outside. At that time I had been pushing for hours. When the head nurse returned she said that Michael's head was in the right place but his body had laid over. That was why he hadn't come. The head nurse saw it as soon as she had lifted the covers, which proved the other nurse just hadn't done her job. Mom had all that on videotape as well.

Once the head nurse took over, she got the doctor in there to examine me. That's when he learned that my blood pressure was sky high. He also said that the baby wasn't in the proper position and both of us were under a lot of stress. That's when he asked my mom to stop videotaping. At this point they didn't know if the baby or I would survive. Then he gave me an epidural to help with the pain. Soon after that I became very calm.   The head nurse worked for quite a while reaching in and turning the baby with every contraction. After several hours of turning, they were able to get him in the right position. Then they wanted me to start pushing. But at that point I was so tired and had so many drugs in my system, I couldn't even feel the contractions anymore. So the nurse said she would tell me when to push.

After much turning and pushing, Michael was finally born around 8:00 pm on March 24, 1989.They started sucking out his lungs when only his head had cleared the canal. After he was completely out of the canal, I didn't hear him crying. I immediately started to panic and asked about him. They kept working on him as they ignored my asking. The minutes seemed like hours, and with every minute that went by, I was asking, why isn't he crying? Finally I heard him cry. Then I could lie back on the bed and take a breath. That was the sweetest music I had ever heard, when I heard his first cry.

I knew that everything would be all right then. I had struggled so much after being in labor for 33 hours. I had burst every blood vessel in my face. I looked like someone had beaten me up. But in an instant, just to hear him cry just washed all that away.

Once they got Michael to breathing okay and got him cleaned up, they put him in my arms. My whole body was so weak and tired that I couldn't even feel him in my arms. I couldn't even feel my arms at that point. I was so afraid; I just knew that I would drop him. But I couldn't give him up just yet. I knew that he was my miracle child.

The next day when mom came in my hospital room, Michael was so vibrant and happy. You would have never known what had transpired the past two days. No one would have ever known how close he and I had come to death. We were so thankful.

Then my mom told me that after receiving such a miracle child that I needed to dedicate him back to God. So I held him up towards the ceiling as an offering unto God. My mom prayed and I repeated the prayer and we dedicated his life back to God in gratitude for what God had done.

Michael was such a blessing to all of us when he was born. My stepfather Sammy had always appeared to everyone like he was a very hardhearted man, but when he held Michael it seemed to just melt his heart and brought out a new person to everyone. From the moment he was born, no matter where Michael was, there seemed to be joy and happiness.

Michael's daddy Tony was in jail at the time he was born. I took Michael to see him when he was only two weeks old. He brought joy to Tony just like he had everyone else. I looked at this as the turning point for Tony to start a new life.

At one point while I was still living with my mom, I was feeding Michael and he got sick. My mom told me to hold his head down so he wouldn't choke. I was doing that, but then he started to have milk come out of his nose. I panicked. Mom jerked him from my arms and held him up by his feet until he stopped getting sick. When it was all over we got a good laugh from it.

I was fortunate when it came to my job also. I worked as a school bus driver for an independent company and could take Michael with me each day. I strapped his car seat on the bus, and he loved being around all of the kids. He won their hearts and they all spoiled him too. He could hold onto his toys and bottle until the kids got on the bus. Then he would constantly drop them so the kids would pick them up and play with him. Smart, so very smart at such a young age.

In 1990 my mom decided that she wanted to move back to Virginia, and so did I. I didn't want to raise my child where there was so much crime and drugs. I felt that a small town like Halifax would be much better. My mom left two weeks before I did and she took Michael with her. I guess Michael was her insurance that I wouldn't change my mind, since his daddy was from Florida. Those two weeks were very hard for me. I couldn't get to Virginia quick enough. During that time my mom lined up a place for us to live once we got there. We settled in and life was good. Michael was so happy.

We lived in a trailer park and my sister would come over every day to watch Michael while I worked. She would take him in the stroller and walk up and down the trailer park with her friends. All of them spoiled him. He loved being outside as well as all of the attention.

Later on that year we moved in with my brother, to share expenses and so Tony would have a ride to work. Michael slept in the same room with his daddy and me. He was such a good child. He hardly ever cried. He could play alone or play with adults or with other children, it didn't matter. He was still happy.

The Christmas of 1990 my mom announced that by the next year she would have a granddaughter. I thought she was talking about my sister, Penny. But I soon learned that it was me that was pregnant again. Just like the first time, I knew what I was having. I knew this time it was a girl.

We moved into a small trailer park with only five trailers and a house. Three of the trailers had older people living in them, and Michael soon won their hearts as well. They would buy special treats for him. They would come out to watch him play outside. Since I was having a hard time with my pregnancy, they helped by watching him.

The guy who lived next door was around my age and would have Michael come over and play video games and give him chips and cookies. Michael loved being around the older generation. He seemed to just take in all of their knowledge. He seemed to enjoy being around them more than he did other kids.

The landlord had a goose that ran free around the trailers. But when it started to chase Michael, the neighbors complained so much that Mr. Ferrell took the goose to the farm. They all seemed to love Michael and would do anything for him. It was almost a competition between the neighbors. They each would buy treats for Michael, trying to outdo the others so Michael would come to their house more often. Michael loved them all. He seemed to always find time to spend with each neighbor.

In 1991 I gave birth to my second miracle child. We named her Michelle. I often referred to Michael and Michelle as my M & M's. Michael loved his sister from the minute that she was born. When he came to the hospital, he was so excited to have a sister. He told all of us that no one could mess with his sister.

We brought Michelle home from the hospital and he didn't want to go anywhere else unless his sister went. He was never really jealous of Michelle. Instead, he would want me to hold both of them. He tried to play with her. When she didn't play back he didn't understand. But when Michelle was a couple of months old, she became more playful. Then Michael would just lie there beside her and let her do whatever she wanted to him.

When Michelle was about six months old, I would get up in the mornings and find Michael in her crib playing with her. It took us a while to figure out how he was getting into her crib. But we learned that he was climbing over the railing to lie next to her. When she woke up, then they would play.

Michael always liked wearing the pajamas with the feet in them. He wanted Michelle to have the same kind. He wanted to do everything with his sister. He never complained about her taking his toys. Lots of times he would bring her his toys to play with. Needless to say, they both loved playing with cars, trucks and little army men. When Michelle got old enough to want to play with dolls, then Michael wanted a doll too. His daddy didn't like that idea too well, but we found Michael a boy doll so he could play dolls with his baby sister. Michael would play for hours with Michelle, putting the babies to sleep, feeding them and taking them outside to play.

Michael was around the age of three when he would help his Papa Sammy work on things. His Papa said he was a fast learner because he had learned all of his tools so quickly. He would run and get tools for his papa. He wanted to help. It didn't matter what his Papa Sammy was doing, he had to help. Sammy would have to give Michael an old board and some nails so he could hammer just like his papa. His Papa Sammy taught him how to work with tools and how to work on things. Michael would be content for hours building stuff or just driving nails in that board.

When his Papa worked on cars or trucks, Michael had to help his Papa do that too. Michael would pretend that he was working on his little cars and trucks or whatever he could find. He loved doing things with his hands.

Michael also wanted to help his Nanny in the kitchen, cooking or baking cookies. When his Nana mowed grass Michael had his little mower out there going up and down the yard just like his Nana. He just wanted to help. He had fun helping people.

When Michael got a little older he started spending more time with his Papa Creasy. Papa Creasy introduced him to the world of hunting and fishing. One time his Papa Creasy took him fishing, and when they got back he couldn't wait for me to come outside and see all of his fish on the ground. He could point out the ones that he had caught and the ones that his papa had caught. Then Papa Creasy started taking Michael with him hunting. Michael would just ride along in his truck. His Papa Creasy would bring him all sorts of snacks and things to eat. Michael enjoyed his time with his papa and loved hunting and fishing.

In 1993 Tony had begun to drink more and became abusive at times. He decided he wanted to move back to Florida. After several instances of abuse toward Michael and me that landed him in court, he felt that was his best option. Michael seemed glad that his daddy was gone, because Tony had started drinking so much and seemed to always be in a bad mood. Michael seemed relieved when his daddy left.

We moved back in with my mom so I could go back to college and earn a degree. I placed Michael and Michelle in daycare. They would enjoy going, but would cry every time that I left them. It finally got to the point that they were afraid that I would not come back. Afraid that I would just leave them like their daddy did. I would have to tell them exactly what time I would be back every day. They would worry the teacher in the afternoons about the time. If I was going to be late, I had to call and let them know or they would be hysterical by the time that I arrived. Whenever Michelle would get upset at daycare, they would have to go get Michael. He would have to come in and calm her down. He was very protective with her. He could always get her to stop crying and make her smile.

As time passed, Michael spent more time with his Papa Creasy going hunting and fishing. He started carrying his own toy gun with him. That's about the time his Papa Creasy started teaching him about guns. He taught him how to use them and how to be careful with them. He also taught him all the safety rules.

By the time Michael was eight years old, his Papa Creasy had bought him a real gun. Oh, what a day that was for Michael! His Papa explained that he could only take it hunting when he went with him. Michael couldn't bring it to his home until after he was about ten years old, but that didn't seem to bother him at all. It was like Michael knew his Papa Creasy just wanted him safe. He didn't whimper or whine about it. He knew he would get to take his gun home when his papa felt that he knew enough to be responsible with it. He had learned to trust his Papa's judgment about guns by then.

By the time Michael was twelve years old, he had shown enough responsibility that he moved up to a bigger gun. We all knew that his passion was hunting and fishing by that age. Michael had even accumulated his own little tackle box for fishing. He would go hunting or fishing every chance that he got.

Michael could learn anything that pertained to work outside or working with his hands, and he learned very quickly. But when it came to books and learning schoolwork, he had a difficult time. At first we thought he just wasn't interested in books. But after awhile we saw how hard he worked at trying to learn his schoolwork. We realized how many hours we spent working with Michael to get him to do thirty minutes of homework. That's when we began to worry that maybe something was wrong. After all, he had almost died at birth. I started paying lots of attention to different things and took notes. After a while I noticed a pattern.

Then I went and asked the school to test him for a learning disability. The teachers were shocked to learn that I had taken notice of so many things. After that, they went over all my notes and agreed that it did sound like some type of learning disability. They set up the test and Michael was tested in the school system. With their test we discovered that he did have a learning problem. They explained it this way: They said his disability was like a picture frame. That Michael could see the frame around the picture, but he could not see the things that made up the picture in the middle. It was the same with words. He could see the word as a whole, but he could not understand how the letters on the inside made up the word. He had a hard time sounding out the letters because he could not put the letters together to form the word. Sounds crazy, doesn't it?

After that Michael was placed in special classes. There he would get more one on one attention. Then he caught on well and did fine with schoolwork. What we didn't understand was when it came to working with his hands or tools, he could learn the most complicated things and remember them, yet had the problem with his words.

Michael was always very helpful in doing things at home around the house. He loved helping his grandparents or simply helping friends. He was also very independent and very protective of his sister and me. He didn't like the fact that I was remarrying. After I did remarry, he didn't get along with his stepfather. He just didn't like him. He would often stand up to him and stand his ground. He was not about to let anyone walk all over him or make him do things he shouldn't.

Michael was very observant. If his stepfather was unfair about a situation, then Michael would let him know about it. He was also very bold and outspoken. He would fuss at Michelle and me because we didn't always speak up, and that upset him. It was around this time that Michael became a little rebellious. Maybe it was his way of getting back at me for getting married, or he was just being a teenager. But I had to come up with some unique ways to punish him. To list a few problems, if I sent him to his room then I would have to lock him in there to keep him there. When I put him in the corner, then I would have to stand over top of him just to make sure he didn't get up until it was time. With Michael his punishment was a little different because I would have to take away his hunting and fishing to get him on track. He was so headstrong about having his way that not too many things worked. He was determined to do things his way, no matter what, most of the time though.

Michael had a fear of thunderstorms that I do remember. Whenever we had a storm, he wanted to be close to me. We would read books or just play to keep his mind off them. If the storm was at night, then the next morning, I would either find him in Michelle's room or on the floor next to my bed. He never really outgrew his fear of storms. But as he got older, they didn't seem to bother him quite as bad.

Then there was the occasion when our neighbor's thirteen-year-old son had locked Michelle inside his house. Michael saw him through the window and saw that he was trying to take her clothes off. He busted through the door, pulled him off Michelle and took her home. Michael never forgot that. He dared that boy to ever set foot anywhere near his sister again. After that, Michael became even more protective of his sister. He was quick to stand up to anyone who even spoke badly about her or me after that.

Michael started working for a friend doing yard work when he was about fourteen years old. At first she would always be there to watch over him and make sure that he did a good job. But after several times of working for her, she could make him a list and then go and take care of other things. She always said that Michael did an excellent job. That he never tried to just slide by doing things halfway. She said she could always count on him to do the job right.

Then Michael got a job at Golden Corral. The managers said that he was a good worker. He said some of the guests would come in and if Michael was cooking, they wanted him to cook their food.

Later on Michael got a job at the scrap yard. This was his favorite job. He would come home so nasty. He worked hard lifting metal and motors or whatever each day, but he loved the work and getting nasty.

He also worked with contractors. He helped build or remodel houses and loved that. He simply enjoyed anything that he could do, as long as it was working with his hands. He didn't mind learning how. He was a good follower when it came to following instructions. He wanted to learn how to do his best, but the hardest thing for him to learn was how to read a tape measure.

As Michael got older, he could have a temper at times. He would always work out his anger by hitting his car, the dashboard or some type of hard object. He even worked out. He got himself a punching bag to work out some of his anger. But he made sure that he never hit a person. When it came to people and their feelings, he was very sensitive. He didn't even like to make anyone mad, for that matter.

I never knew Michael to start a fight, but he wouldn't back down from one either if someone was dumb enough to throw a lick. He lifted weights and kept himself strong and fit, and he knew how strong he was and he would stand his ground. Other people knew he was strong also. Most of the time they would back down. He never really had to show how strong he was. He tried to talk it through and settle it peacefully. Michael was a teenager, but he had times that he was angry or upset about things, just like any other teen. But most of the time he was a very loving and very caring person.

Michael ended his conversations with "I love you." He wasn't embarrassed to let people, not even his friends, know how he felt about his family and friends. He always made sure when he talked to me on the phone he ended it, I love you. When he was leaving, he would say to me, I love you Mom. When he talked to his Nana he would end it with, Love you Nana. If it was his Papa, Jay, Penny, whoever, his last words were going to be, I Love you. He loved animals, too. He had several dogs, a snake, a hamster, and even a rat as his pets. Like I said, he was a unique son, brother, grandson, nephew, and friend. He was born with that loving and joyful personality that drew people to him like a magnet.

Michael also had some rough times. Times when he started drinking, taking pills and smoking pot. Like most teens, he had to try it. Like most moms, I didn't like it. He went through a spell where he wasted his money on that stuff and partying with his friends, but it didn't last long. He soon learned that if he wanted anything out of this life, he had to be responsible. He learned what being responsible meant. Then he worked so he would have money and not waste it. A lesson he learned in a few short years. Some people don't learn it in a lifetime. He knew his family wasn't proud of him for doing the drugs, but he decided on his own to turn his life around.

If he was short on money, he took on extra work. He would work in other people's yards to make extra cash. He would sell scrap metal on the side to pick up a few extra bucks. He would do anything anyone needed him to do. But he also found time to help someone else, whether it was a stranger or a friend who needed him. If they paid him it was all right, but if they didn't, he didn't complain. By the time Michael was eighteen he had realized that he had to work for what he wanted. He had realized that in order to get a good paying job, then he had to leave the drinking, pills, and pot alone.

After he turned eighteen, he got a good paying job at Dollar General. He had dreams of owning his own home. He wanted so much for something to be his. He was willing, at this point, to work hard to have it. Determined to meet his dreams by working for it himself.

The house next door came open, and he figured out a way to buy it. Michael would eat oodles of noodles for a week just to make sure he could pay the payment and light bill. Unless he came to my house or went to his Aunt Penny's to eat, which he did often. He lived without TV except for recorded or rented movies, but he was happy! He was so happy that he had something he could call his. He would tickle me by calling and asking me to come next door to see if what he was cooking looked right or if he was doing it right. When he ran low on groceries, then he shopped at Mama's kitchen. He would come to mama's cupboard and see what he could take home. Michael wanted his house to be decorated his way. He decorated it with his deer heads, deer pictures, and pictures of family members, and he made sure that it was a manly-looking house.

I remember when he pierced his tongue. I got home and he was in the yard. He called me over to the edge of my yard and his. He wrapped his arms around me and told me he loved me. Then he said he wanted to show me something. As he was holding me tight he stuck out his tongue and laughed. He knew that I wouldn't like it, and he wanted to be close to his house in case he needed to run real quick.

Michael appeared to be manly and bold on the outside to those who didn't know him. But if you dug deep into what he had kept from his childhood, you would find that he was very sentimental. He kept things like his toy guns, his cars and his games. He kept pictures of family in his wallet. He kept the little doll that we used when he was a baby, which held his bottle up, while we were driving down the road. He kept certain toys that were given to him as presents that he wouldn't let other kids play with because he wanted to keep them just like they were. Michael was very sensitive when it came to his family also.

When his cousin JoJo died, Michael took it very hard. He tried not to let others see his emotions. He thought he had to be strong for his Aunt Penny and Nana. But when his Papa Creasy died, he didn't care who saw him cry. He was hurting deep at the loss of his papa. He loved his family and friends and wanted to be close to all of them all the time.

Michael always made sure he attended family functions and was usually the first to arrive. He loved being around his family. He loved spending time with his little cousins Alexis and Jayden. He would babysit for them and let them spend the night with him. He made sure that he had toys at his house for them to play with when they came over. We went camping one year with his Aunt Penny, Uncle Kenneth, Alexis and Jayden, his sister and me. He had a good time and wanted to do things with his cousins. He never fussed because they woke him up early or wanted to go walking with him.

Michael hunted every opportunity that he got and brought home plenty of meat to put in the freezer. He learned how to cook deer meat and even made deer jerky. Michael even took the risk of driving off the road when he started driving, to hit a deer on purpose, just so he could have the meat. He came home late one night and woke me up to take pictures of an albino deer that he had hit with his car. It is a wonder that any car lasted with Michael driving it. He would purposefully hit deer, birds, raccoons, or whatever crossed his path while driving.

When it was the right time, he would go fishing. He sometimes would fish all night long. He enjoyed spending time with his friends and catching fish. There were many occasions that Michael would come home late at night and wake me up so that I could take pictures of his fish.

I remember when I took Michael to buy his first truck. I didn't think too much of the truck. But he kept pointing out all of the good things about it and how he could use it for hunting and fishing. We bought it. I watched him driving it from the rearview mirror all the way home, and he was smiling like a possum. He would rev up the motor just to hear it be loud. He would go outside and crank the truck just to hear it run. He was like a little kid that had just received a million dollars. Once Michael set his heart on something, he would do whatever he could to get it.

Another time when Michael was younger, I remember he wanted to play football. Something else I didn't want him to do out of fear of him being hurt, because I felt it was such a rough sport. Therefore I conveniently missed the sign up times every time. But Michael soon learned what I was doing and signed himself up. Then told me that I had to pay the fees. I went to the games but closed my eyes a lot, because he always seemed to be on the bottom of the pile.

Michael also played T-ball when he was small all the way up to when he could play Dixie Youth baseball. Just as soon as he was old enough, he signed up for that. I loved watching him play baseball. There were many occasions that I would have to make arrangements to take Michael to a ball game, then rush to take Michelle somewhere else to play softball. We stayed on the go all the time with sports, family and friends. Many days I felt like their taxi driver, but it was one of the greatest pleasures of my life. It gave us time to talk or just listen to their favorite music. In a car with those two was a trip in itself. I would take him to his friend's house. Another adventure, because it seemed like every friend of his always lived much further out in the country than we did. Many happy memories in those trips also.

Michael always had a flair for the girls. He started having girlfriends in kindergarten. He never had any trouble finding a girlfriend. Even his female teachers loved his attitude and the way he carried himself. His teachers would always say that they would help him in any way they could. Michael didn't have any trouble making friends, either. When he found a true friend he would stand by them, no matter what. His friends and family were his whole life. He cherished friendship the same way he cherished family, with lots of love and respect.

I remember in May 2008 I was graduating from Averett University. Michael picked on me for having to get up so early to go to graduation. He was the first one ready that morning. To me he seemed to be so proud of his mom. After graduation, everyone was suppose to meet outside. He almost ran people over so he could be the first one outside to meet me. He ran up to me and hugged me. Then he said for me to hurry up because he wanted to be the first one to take a picture with me, too. He was so full of life and happiness. So happy for anyone that accomplished anything. We all took lots of pictures that day. One of my favorite memories is how hard he worked to be the first one to take a picture with me that day. I will always remember that one.

I have only shared a few highlights of my son's life. To write all he meant to me would take volumes of books. But at this time it is all I feel I can share with you. I sincerely hope I haven't bored you. If you only knew how painful it was to share a little, or how many tears I've cried to get these few little words written down. I know every mom in this country could talk for days and weeks about their children and I hope you do. I hope you cherish your children every day you have them with you. And I would like to think that no other family would ever have to suffer through the death of a child. But I'm afraid that won't happen as long we live on earth with so much jealousy and hatred.

I was blessed in my life to have two miracle children who have given me so much joy and happiness. It is with much sadness that I had to relinquish my first child back to God so early in his life. It has been very difficult learning how to live without him in my life. Every inch of my life was filled with my kids. Everything I did was for them. Every dream was around them. I made mistakes. I didn't always get it right, but I always loved my children. I know the life I had with both of my children for nineteen years will be cherished all the days of my life. Just as surely as we made those memories together inch by inch. It will take me a lifetime to learn how to live without him on this earth. But I take it one day at a time. Some days are better than others.

I have struggled with anger, resentment, sadness, depression and happiness. I know that Michael is in a much better place, but I also know life without him is a struggle. He will always be remembered and missed. I still have days that I can talk about him and smile, remembering all of the good times. But then again I can talk about those same memories and just cry. No one knows what it is like to lose a child unless they have lived through it. It is a devastating experience.

I live each day now knowing that he is with my daddy, my grandparents, my uncle, my aunt, my nephew and all of my other family members that have gone on to be with the Lord. I have peace knowing where he is. And I have peace knowing that he came back to us on the day of his funeral. He made sure he

71

made himself seen at the graveside in a picture. How? I really don't know. Someone else took the picture and when I saw it, I couldn't believe my own eyes at first. He made sure that he was seen in that picture so clearly that there wouldn't be any mistake in seeing him. He wanted all of us to know that he was there. I take that picture and look at it every day. I can see his face in it every day and I know in my heart he watches over his family and friends. I know he is happy and he is rejoicing with our heavenly Father.

I luv ya son, is how we ended all of our conversations. And that will never change, Michael.

Love, your mom,
Tammy Johns Hayes

Michael so proud of his Mama, April 2008.

Michael, His Mama Tammy & Sister Michelle Ann (Chell)
His whole life was family, friends, hunting, fishing and
LIFE!
Michael Loved Life!
And
Life loved Michael!

Tammy, Michael, Papa Creasy

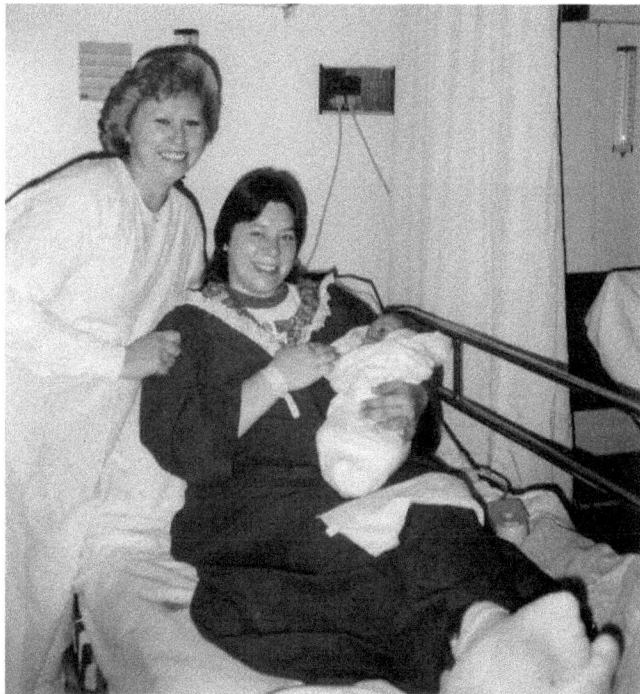

Proud Nana, Mama, Michael
March 24th 1989

Nov. 1991
Shaving with Daddy.

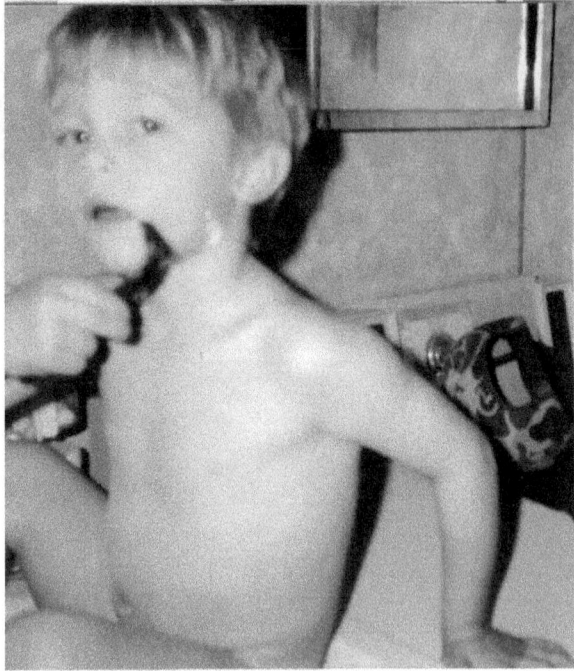

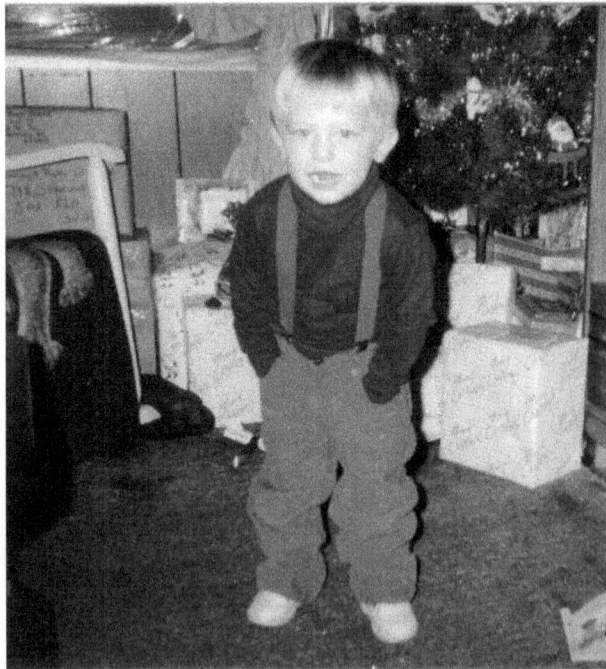

A Mama's Boy!

Daddy Teaching Son How To Shoot A Gun!

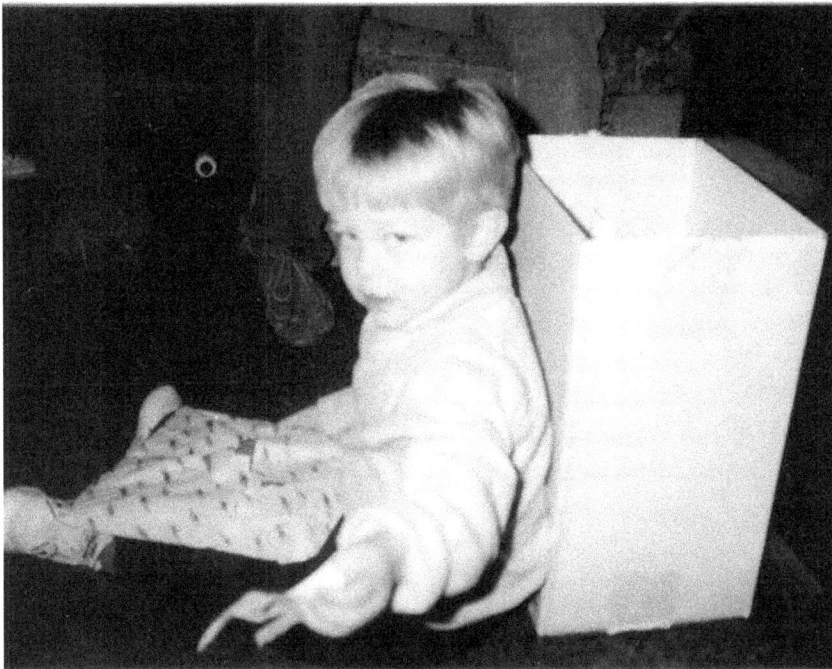

One Year Old, He Threw His Trash Away!

Born To Fish!

Mama, Michael, Michelle
My Son, My Daughter, I Luv You!

CHAPTER EIGHT

FROM THE EYES OF HIS SISTER, MICHELLE ANN JOHNS

CHAPTER EIGHT

FROM THE EYES OF HIS SISTER, MICHELLE ANN JOHNS

Michael was only two and a half years old when I was born. I was told when Nana brought him to see Mama and me in the hospital, he got on the bed beside Mama so he could see me. I had both of my fists balled up like most babies do, so Michael balled up his and started hitting my fists. He was ready to play. Of course Mama and everybody else there jumped on him, telling him not to hurt me. But he didn't understand. Nana took a picture of it and we have had lots of laughs over the years over that first visit.

I was told at first he was jealous of me and started doing baby things again. But it didn't take long for him to grow out of it. I was also told that when my daddy left, I was about two years old. That the first thing Michael said to me was, It's okay Chell, you can talk now. He said that because my daddy would get mad when he couldn't understand me, so I wouldn't talk to anyone but Mike.

Ever since that day my brother has been there for me and protected me. So I guess you can say he was a daddy figure toward me. My big brother Michael was also famous for giving me my nickname, "Chell." He never could quite say Michelle when he was little because he lost his front teeth, so he just called me Chell. Mike was good at giving nicknames. Our grandmother was babysitting him one day and Mike was trying to ask for a banana, but the way it came out was nana. So our grandmother thought that was what he was calling her. Ever since that day, she has gone by Nana or Nanny to all the grandkids.

Michael and I would go visit our Papa Creasy all the time. Papa taught us both how to fish and would take us all the time. We also enjoyed helping Papa feed the chickens and dogs that he had. One day we were helping Papa fix one of the chicken pens when Mike picked up something off the ground and asked what it was. Papa turned around and said, "That's chicken manure."

Mike looked at Papa funny and said, "What's that mean?"

Papa Creasy laughed and said, "Chicken shit."

I have never seen Michael drop something so fast and wipe his hands on his pants.

When we were little, it was nothing for Mama to get up and find me in Mike's bed. I was always getting scared when I woke up in the middle of the night, so I would go get in the bed with Michael.

When we lived in Georgia, Mike said he always knew when I was coming to get in the bed with him because he would hear me running up the hallway. Then hear me kick the coffee table and say, "Shit." Then I would jump in the bed.

One of our favorite things to do together was play fighting. If someone was to walk in there, that didn't know us, they would probably think we were really fighting. Mike and I knew each other's limitations and knew how much each could take. Now I'm not saying we never hurt each other. But we were pretty good about knowing when to stop.

One time Mike and I were at Nanny's house playing pool in the dayroom with a friend. It was Mike and our friend's turn to play. But Mike was a better player so he decided to take the eight ball off the table. This way the friend wouldn't have to worry about making the eight ball before it was time to. I was sitting on the couch and Mike thought I was looking, so he tossed the ball to me. I never saw it coming until it hit me in the eye. Of course it gave me a black eye and we knew we were going to get in trouble. Michael and I knew as soon as Nanny found out that we would be grounded from playing pool for a while. So we thought up this plan to tell Nanny and Mama. We told them that Mike accidentally shot it off the table and it just so happened to hit me in the eye. They believed it and we didn't get grounded.

After Mike passed away, I told the truth and Nanny said she probably would have grounded us.

Another time Mama kept smelling something in her bedroom. She asked Mike to look under her bookshelf and see if he saw anything. After looking, he said it was a dead rat. So he got a wooden gun to stick under there to pull it out. Then he handed the wooden gun to me, and grabbed the rat with the pliers. Mike thought he was going to be funny and try to put the dead rat in my face. But out of reflex I smacked him on the side of the face with the wooden gun. After that day he never tried to chase me with a dead rat again.

When we were in elementary school we would go to Nanny's every day after school until Mama got off of work. One day we were riding bikes with some friends. We would take turns racing each other down a paved hill. I was racing this other guy one day and ended up falling. I rolled all the way down the hill. I had a big goose egg on my head, scraped my knee, and messed up my elbow. That night when we went home, my brother was so nice to me. He made sure I had enough pillows to prop up my arm. He brought me a TV tray and then brought me my supper. Mike was even nice enough to stop eating and fix me a drink and a little more food.

Ever since I was little, every time I'd go fishing with Michael he would baby me. He would bait my hook and even take the fish off the hook for me. Sometimes he would throw the line out for me if we were around some trees or something. No matter what he was doing, he would stop and help me if I needed it.

One year we took a trip to our cousins Jessie and Jo's house to go fishing. They lived on the James River. When we were fishing up there, Mike was babying me just like he always did, but so was Jessie. I don't think I would have had to do anything unless I just wanted to. We caught close to seventy croakers that year. We had so much fun fishing and visiting with Jessie and Jo.

When I met my boyfriend and we went fishing together, he didn't baby me. So I finally learned how to do it myself.

The whole way through elementary school Michael acted like he didn't know me, like most brothers do. But that all changed when I got to high school. Michael was ready to quit school by that time. But he went back one semester, which was my freshman year, just to make sure everyone knew he was my big brother. He would talk to me and even give me a hug in the hallway. He quit after that semester. But he still had friends there to watch over me. Those friends told him one day that a girl that rode the bus beside mine had called me some ugly names. So one evening I was on my bus and saw Mike go on the other bus beside mine. I was looking all around like what's going on, because I had no idea. He went on that bus and told that girl that she had better stop talking about me. That he couldn't hit her because she was a girl, but he had friends that would. I never heard anything else out of that girl.

My whole life, anytime I had a problem or needed to talk about something, I would go talk to Michael. A lot of people might have thought that Michael was just a crazy teenager who didn't have good advice, but to me, they were wrong. Because when I talked to him he would be serious and tell me what he thought about the situation. He would add in something funny sometimes to make me laugh. But he always had something serious with it.

The last year or so that Mike was alive, we kinda grew apart. His girlfriend seemed jealous of mine and Mike's relationship. Every time I would try to talk to him about something personal, she would have to know what we talked about. It tore me up inside that I couldn't talk to him whenever I wanted to any more. But I was trying to be nice and not cause any problems between them, so I said nothing.

On Saturday, June 21, 2008, I was at my aunt's house for a party. I saw Michael there, but really didn't talk to him. We spoke when we got there, but that was it. I left and went back to my boyfriend's house. There I got a call and was told to come home. From that moment on my life had drastically changed. Sometimes I feel I don't know where to go from here. But I just take one day at a time and rely on the fact that I know Michael is still here watching over me.

That's all I can share at this time because it just hurts so much to know my brother was taken from me out of rage and jealousy.

I love you, big brother. I will always know you are here with me.

Love your Lil sis Chell,

Michelle Ann Johns

Michael & Michelle!

Mama, Daddy, Michael & Michelle
My Family!

Michael, his Mama Tammy, his Nana Carolyn, his Great-Grandmother Geneva &
Michael's Great-Great Grandmother Falls in 1990

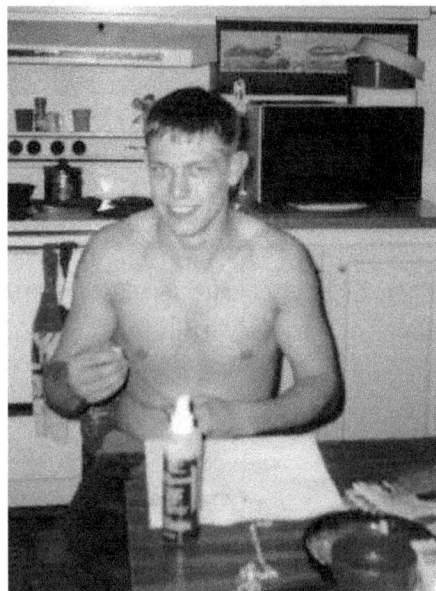

Michael getting ready for the Prom! April 2008

"I Love You, Michael!

Thank You Big Brother For Never Leaving Us!

CHAPTER NINE

FROM THE EYES OF HIS AUNT PENNY

Michael & Aunt Penny!

CHAPTER NINE

FROM THE EYES OF HIS AUNT PENNY

I was twelve years old when my nephew Michael was born. It was an exciting and happy day for our family. I was an aunt. How great was that? Little did I know the joy that he would bring to me in his short life here on earth.

Michael and his mother, my sister Tammy, lived with us after he was born for a while. A living, breathing baby doll. Oh wow! I held him and fed him. He was mine, or at least that is what I pretended. I remember he would be sleeping and his mom would be busy and tell me not to wake him. But as soon as she'd leave the room I'd wake him and say, "He woke up, Sissy." She never got angry with me. That's just the way she was.

As Michael got older, we had moved to Virginia. I stayed with Tammy, Tony and Michael until Mom got settled in the house. My friends and I would push Michael in his stroller all around the trailer park. He loved it and we loved him. I hardly went anywhere that he didn't go with me. He was always so happy just to be able to go with me and my friends. We didn't mind having him with us, either. He was such a happy baby.

As I got older and became a teenager, my life was busier. Michael didn't live with us any more but he didn't live far either. I would still babysit him and saw him a lot. He had a sister in 1991 and he loved her so much. He watched over her and did until the day he passed from his physical body. A born protector of her!

Michael loved to play ball and hunt. He played football also and was very good at anything he played. We attended every game no matter what he was in at the time, even other family members and friends like Twila were there. He carried his own audience and cheerleading team with him. He lived a very lively and happy life surrounded by family and friends.

He liked scary movies. I remember one night he wanted to watch a scary movie. We tried to get him to take a shower first, then watch the movie, but of course, he couldn't wait. He had to see the movie first, then take his shower. As always, we gave in. He had a gift of persuading you to get his way. After we watched the scary movie he went to take his shower. He was so scared. When he got in the shower he wouldn't close the curtain. When I went in and saw the curtain opened I couldn't resist. I stepped up, and said 'BOO'! I scared him so bad, he almost jumped out of the shower.

I have many such memories with Michael. Every detail of his life is nothing but good memories. He never caused any problems or made any bad memories with me. I will cherish them all for my entire life and share them with my children or with anyone that wants to listen. He was such a good-hearted person with such deep feelings. I thought that made him unusual. But that's the way Michael was. He made everyone he was around feel special and loved.

In school his teachers and fellow students loved him. Every class with every teacher, they gave us a good report. They said he was a good student. Worked hard and got along well with other students. His family was there for every school function to support him and listen to his teachers brag on him.

As he got older I remember him struggling with some of his classes in school. I gave him some advice about working hard in school and that it would be worth it in the end. He always listened to my advice. He never argued with me. Whether he used it or not is another story. But what teenager uses all the advice they get from adults, especially adults who themselves had made a lot of mistakes in their own life?

When they moved to Georgia, it felt like I had lost them. They weren't up the street anymore. They weren't coming by to visit every day. It was heart breaking for Michael, Michelle, and myself. Family was all they had known. And they had moved to a place with no family. It hurt them very deeply. But soon his mother realized she needed family and we needed them, so they moved back to Virginia. After that, I think Michael and Michelle appreciated family even more. They made sure they attended every function and gathering with family. When other teenagers would be busy with teen stuff, they never made anything more important than family.

He loved living on the farm and never left it after that. Hunting was a passion for him, and he didn't kill a bird without having to show it to me. He was a great hunter. He lived to hunt anything that moved. And he was good at it. A lot of mornings if I knew he was out hunting and I had cooked a big breakfast, I would call him and he would come down to my house and eat.

To this day when I cook a big breakfast I think of him. I cry often, and long to have him sitting there at my table eating with us again.

Michael adored my children Alexis and Jayden just as much as I adored him. He was there for the birth of all three of my children. I remember like yesterday him playing and talking baby talk to them. My second child, Joseph, who we called JoJo, was stillborn and Michael took that very hard. He was such a compassionate boy and kept that compassion as he became a man. He would play with my girls and they loved him dearly.

My youngest daughter Jayden was one week from her second birthday when Michael left us, and she remembers him fondly. Michael was proud of them. He would show them off to his friends. He even carried their pictures in his wallet, and placed their pictures on his walls. He was never Cousin Michael. He was Uncle Michael to them.

When Michael moved into his own place, he was so excited. He was still on the farm with his mom, me, and his Uncle Jay. He couldn't even wait for Old Dominion to turn his lights on. He pulled a heavy-duty drop cord from his mama's house to his just so he could be over there. That was the funniest thing! To see that old orange cord running from his mama's to his house. That's how excited he was to take ownership of his own home.

I called him one morning before he moved in and asked him if he was busy. He said no, so I went and picked him up and took him to town. I bought him one hundred dollars worth of groceries for his new home. I had never seen him so happy. He was telling everyone about all of the groceries he got. He was so appreciative of anything you did for him. We went to some different stores and he bought some silverware and other household stuff. A nineteen-year-old man buying household stuff! But he wanted his home so badly. He wanted to be on his own, furnish it and decorate it. That was a proud day for me also. I was so excited for him.

He moved his stuff in and decorated it himself, and it was unbelievably gorgeous. He had his living room decorated with his trophy deer and turkey beards. It was just the best! And Michael had to invite us over to show it off. We were very proud. He kept it clean, the grass mowed, and cooked his own meals. He even invited people over to eat with him. He was just not typical for a nineteen-year-old boy. My girls, Alexis and Jayden, even spent the night with him a couple of times. For the first couple of weeks, except to go to work, I don't think he left his home very much. His home was one of his dreams come true and he enjoyed being there. Michael only got to live a few months in his dream home.

June 21st, 2008, I would have to say was one of the worst days of my life. I was having a cookout for my son Jo Jo that had passed away June 17th, 2005. Michael was invited of course, as well as, the rest of the family. I called Michael at twelve noon to see what time he was coming down. He said he was going to get up, take a shower, brush his teeth and he would be down in a little while. I said okay.

People started arriving around two pm, I guess. We had cooked a bunch of food, hamburgers, hotdogs, deer meat, crawdads and all the fixings. When Michael got there, we were just starting to eat. He fixed his plate, enough for three. My cousin Kristi even asked him if he got enough.

He laughed and said, "Yep." He took his plate outside and ate at the table with some other family members. Michael always did love to eat.

After eating he chased the kids with the water hose, spraying and laughing as they ran from him. Alexis and Jayden thought that was the grandest thing for Michael to play with them. We all sat outside watching and laughing at the kids playing, talking, joking and laughing with one another. We were having a good time. It was a good day.

Later that day close to evening, people started gradually leaving. My sister Tammy, Michael's mother, told Michael she loved him and she'd see him tomorrow as she left. As time passed it was down to just a few people, Michael, my brother, his wife all the kids and us. It was around 7:30 pm and Michael was ready to go. He had brought his girlfriend with him and they were going to walk home, but my husband Kenneth offered them a ride. Michael said goodbye, and they left...

Little did I know that would be the last time I would see Michael alive in his body. Little did I know that was the last time any of us would see him alive...

I was one of the last people to see and talk to Michael, besides Kenneth who took them home, and his girlfriend who was in the house at the time of his death.

I was one of the first people to be notified by a friend and neighbor that he had been shot.

I was the one who had to call his Nana, his mama and his sister.

When a grandparent dies, it is sad. When a parent dies it is even more sad. But there is no explanation of the pain when a young, healthy, good, happy person is taken away from you. It is like ripping the life right out of you.

A piece of me died when Michael passed. A piece of Alexis died when Michael passed. A piece of Jayden died when Michael passed.

Words cannot explain the hurt and pain. No one could ever take his place in our heart. The gift of life given to us was taken from us, in just a split second, a happy, well adjusted, loving, caring young man stolen from us.

It is amazing to me how much we can love someone. Amazing how much we take for granted the days and times we spend with them. But when they die, you always wish you had more time. I think about the families who only see each other a couple of times a year or less. They could see each other more or as often as they like, but refuse to take the time.

I am so thankful for every moment I get with family now. I am so thankful for every hug, every phone call, every hello, every goodbye, and every 'I love you'.

I think of Michael every day, some days more than others, a deer in the field that doesn't seem scared. A flickering light, a refreshing breeze, even the wind blowing through my hair I know it's Michael. He's just letting us know he's still with us. His spirit lives on. He's everywhere. He's here!

How much time is enough to spend with a loved one? If I had spent every waking moment with Michael, would it have been enough? No, it wouldn't have been. Why? Because love is something you can never get enough of.

Did Michael know that was the last time he'd ever be in the flesh body with us? I don't think so. Did Michael know when he stepped in his own front door and walked down that hall into his bedroom, that it would be the last time? No! I don't think so.

In my opinion he was taken from us out of jealousy. He didn't just leave us. He would never just leave us. Some people hate so deeply, they go into a rage when they see someone else so loved, as Michael was.

How do I describe my life as Michael's aunt? Joyful! Blessed! Loved! Proud! Honored! Just to say the least..... He gave us nothing but Joy, Blessings, Love, and Respect. "I am honored to have known you as my first nephew, Michael Lee Johns!"

Love your Aunt Penny

Michael loving his Aunt Penny

Michael had many little dolls, as mentioned in this book,
Even a Santa Claus baby

Michael looking so proud holding his sister, Michelle

One of Michael and Michelle's school pictures
Mama's M & M's

MICHAEL L. JOHNS

Scottsburg, VA Little League Football Team

Michael holding his first little cousin, Alexis, sitting beside his Aunt Penny

Michael and his little cousin, Jayden, camping at
Thousand Trails Campsite in Rustburg, VA and having a blast.

Michael's Last Family Reunion with some of his cousins of his generation
The Annual Smith Family Reunion in June 2008!

Michael and one of his favorite teachers at Sinai Elementary, Miss Williams! She was his fifth grade teacher.

Michael and one of his big catfish that he caught in 2003

CHAPTER TEN

FROM THE EYES OF HIS UNCLE JAY

When Michael lived with his Uncle Jay in 1990

Uncle Jay introducing Michael to his first motorcycle in 1990

Michael showing off his catch of the day

As you can see, he never changed

Michael and Uncle Jay at the Fourth of July, Scottsburg, VA annual parade

CHAPTER TEN

FROM THE EYES OF HIS UNCLE JAY

Being Michael's uncle made me proud. He was always a good kid. I lived with Tammy and Tony when Michael was growing up. He was like my son. I took him fishing and hunting and he loved it.

I remember when he killed his first deer. We were hunting behind my house next to the beaver pond. I jumped up this nice eight-point buck. I shot him in the butt, but he kept running. Then I yelled, "Here he comes, Michael."

Michael ran about six hundred yards or more to get the shot. When I got to him, I said, "Did you get him?"

Michael was standing over the deer with the barrel of the gun right on the deer. He said, with the gun pointing right at the deer shaking like a leaf on a tree, "I hit him. But he's not getting away." Michael didn't realize the deer was dead.

I laughed so hard I just about cried. It made me so happy to see that look on his face when he realized he had killed the deer. After that day, Michael was hooked. He hunted every day no matter how cold it was.

Soon he was killing more deer than I was. He made me so proud. He would bring the deer to my house for me to see his kill, and brag a little, with that little shit-eating grin he always had.

One day I was sick, and Michael and Kenneth came by to get my four-wheeler. When they came back about two hours later they had a nice buck on it. The very one I had shot at earlier. That made me even sicker then. He had killed my buck. "Aw, man, you killed my buck." Michael just grinned.

Michael went with me to the hunting club. He would always ride with me. But when we got hungry we always knew to call daddy (Papa Creasy) on the radio. Daddy always kept crackers and potted meat. Michael really enjoyed hunting with the club. He always got along with everybody.

Michael never met a stranger he didn't like. In a way, he was a little bit like me in that. Other people used to say he looked a lot like me too. That always made me feel good. I guess I re-lived my life through Michael. I think that's what hurt so bad when he left us June 21st 2008. A big part of me died that day.

I remember a time when I used to let Michael ride my four-wheeler. This one time I heard he was rough on it and he lost the tail light. I told him when he found the tail light, he could ride it again. He never asked to ride it again.

Another time he killed a deer and he dragged it all the way to the house. He was too proud, or respectful of me, to ask me if he could use the four-wheeler to bring it to the house.

As Michael got older I started letting him drive my truck. He came back one day and I asked him where my truck was. He looked at me and said, "I turned it over."

I said, "Are you hurt?

He said, "No, not right now."

Later I heard that Michael told Kenneth that he was coming to tell me about wrecking my truck and it was the hardest thing he ever had to do. Michael said he would pay for my truck to get it fixed, but I never made him.

Michael was always helping me. He was always willing to do his part to lend a helping hand. He never missed a family get-together or a chance to help any family member. Also, he knew there would be plenty of food, and he loved to eat. He could always put some food away. He always looked out for his family, especially his mom and little sister.

I miss him just as much today as I did the day he left us. When I need help around the house, I still look for him. Then I remember. I will always think about Michael first because he was always there, and then I have to remind myself he's not here. It's just hard to image that.

When Michael first passed away I could feel his presence on the farm. When I left for work every night, I would look for him on the side of the road or in the yard because I knew he would be there. But now I look on the side of the road and in the yard wishing I could see him again. I still look.

Michael and I never showed each other much emotion. We were too manly to hug or tell each other how much we loved each other. I wish I had told him more so I would have heard him tell me he loved me. We knew how we felt about each other, but now I see how important it is to tell your loved ones every day that you love them.

Every day in the woods or in my truck on my way to work, I think of him and I tell him I love him. It's not the same, but it makes me feel better to do it anyway.

People say time heals all things, all wounds, but time hasn't healed my heart yet. I still hurt as much today as I did that day.

I can't wait to get to heaven and see all of my loved ones again and tell them how much I've missed them. Just to tell them how much I love them face to face again.

I love you Michael.

Love from your, Uncle Jay

One of Michael's big bucks that he killed and mounted

Just one proud day of hunting. Anyone that knew him knew he loved to hunt!

Does this buck look familiar, Uncle Jay?

What about this albino one, Uncle Jay?

Michael at Uncle Jay's, with his famous grin

PART TWO

From The Eyes of Christine Creasy (Jay's wife)

From The Eyes of Christine Creasy (Jay's wife)

I had only known Michael for a couple of years. I started dating his Uncle Jay in January of 2006. I didn't know Michael as much as I would've enjoyed. I've seen Michael go from being a young eighteen-year-old living at home with his mother and sister, who were the center of his life, to living on his own next door to them.

I heard many stories about Michael and Michelle on how close they were. How if you picked on one, you picked on both. You could say he was close to his Aunt Penny and her husband Kenneth also. When he wasn't at work or out with his friends, he would be at Penny's playing with Alexis and Jayden or just hanging out.

Now I tell you, when it came to hunting and fishing, Michael would always outdo his Uncle Jay and Kenneth. It wouldn't be anything to look out the window and see Michael cleaning a deer, or finding a catfish head in our yard. Michael would be the first one to get a deer during hunting season.

Jay would be like man, I gotta get one bigger than that now, bigger than what he got. Jay would walk around the house going on and on about it. I thought it was so funny how Michael beat them every year with the biggest deer or the biggest fish.

I remember Austin the first time he watched Michael cleaning a deer. Our son looked like he was going to get sick at any minute, but he didn't. Michael thought it was kinda funny and started telling Austin stories of him and his Papa Creasy and Uncle Jay and when they took him hunting.

When they would talk about Austin not being quiet when he was hunting, Michael would grin and say, "I was the same way." Then he told Jay that he needed to take some snacks with him and it would be alright. Michael told Austin he remembered when he used to talk too much, and his Papa Creasy took snacks for him to eat to keep him quiet. So he reminded Jay what to do and how to teach Austin to be quiet when hunting. Michael had a lot of good advice for Austin when he hung around him.

Michael was starting to change more from being a regular teenager to a young man getting more responsible. Getting a better job and moving out from his mother's and into his own place. He had started taking care of himself and his girlfriend. It was good that he didn't have to move far away where he couldn't see his mother and sister every day, or his Aunt Penny and Uncle Jay, because he moved next door to his mom.

I'm sure he was very proud of his accomplishments on a big move in his life like that. I know his family was right there to help him in any way. To be eighteen and already buying his own land and home was a great jump. And I'm sure he was scared at the same time.

I know I was very proud of Michael getting his life on track and really wanting something out of his life. He set good examples for his little cousins by doing that.

Our kids, Austin, Wyatt, Kalee and Jayson really loved Michael. Just the times they could spend with him or see him meant a lot to them. Michael was still young enough to play with his nieces and nephews, he called them, and not act like he was too old.

I'm sure he could have given a lot of good advice and shared his own experiences he had lived in his life with the younger ones when the time came. It is sad that the younger ones will miss out on that now.

Michael had a picture of Alexis, Jayden and Jayson on his nightstand by his bed. I thought that was unusual for a nineteen-year-old, but that was Michael. He carried pictures in his wallet of all his nieces and nephews. Also something not too many teens would do.

I think about the way he drove his car and how loud his music was. I think about the times he came home late. Then I think of what is in store for me when our children hit those teenage years, especially our three boys. Then I wish Michael was still here so he could help our children through some of their teen years and share his stories. Maybe, just maybe, they would have listened and be spared some heartaches. Just the little he shared with them, they listened. So I feel he could have taught them a lot.

I remember when Michael took his girlfriend to the prom. Michelle and her boyfriend Jonathan went, and they did the whole thing together. How lucky and awesome was that?

Michelle always talking about how smart Michael was, just as much as he talked about how smart she was. Michael was always talking about how smart Michelle was, bragging about her going to college and making something of herself. I remember him looking at Michelle and smiling at her, for her accomplishments so far.

Michael wouldn't say much around me. He was kinda quiet, but always funny. He had such a big heart. He loved going to family functions, especially the food. Michael would say you get your best food at the Smith family reunion at J.P.'s every first Sunday of June.

Now when his mom cooked, you had a feast also. Her baked beans, green beans and potatoes are to die for, and his Nana's banana pudding, he said.

He was right, too. His Mama, Nana and Aunt Penny always made sure that there was enough food for Michael to eat later, and there always was. Michael knew he would have plenty of leftovers to eat for a few days. His mama, Aunt Penny and Nana would make sure of that. Michael could eat. I don't know where he put it all when he ate, because he was thin and kinda tall.

Michael was very sure of himself and had a lot of self-confidence. He was loved by his whole family and had been all his life, and had so much love in himself to give out.

I know I will always keep Michael in my heart. Just something as simple as a word or a Christmas bag or just a smell brings back a flood of memories. So he really didn't go anywhere. Little things, like a word spoken by someone, or a Christmas bag or a certain smell, little things like that, just let you know that he is still around in our hearts and minds. He will never leave this farm, he loved it too much. I love you Michael.

Michael dancing with his sister Michelle at her sweet sixteen party!
"I would like to remember Michael and the way he loved his Mama and sister,"
Christine said.
Love from Christine

Papa Creasy starting to teach Michael his hunting lessons

April 2008
I wonder if there is hunting and fishing in heaven?
I sure hope so!

Michael's first car

Michael with just one of many Turkeys!

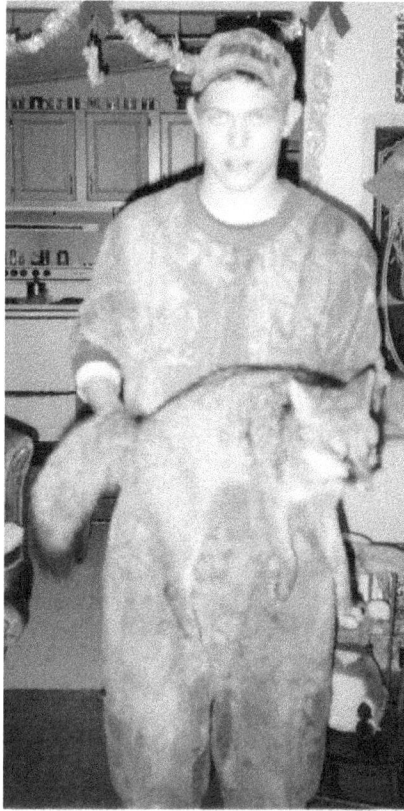

Michael with his fox

Michelle and Jonathan all dressed up ready to go to the prom. They are waiting for Michael to hurry up and get dressed. He is procrastinating, as much as he can, because he hates wearing a tuxedo. Then they will go and enjoy the night at Halifax County High School Prom.

CHAPTER ELEVEN

FROM THE EYES OF TWO BEST FRIENDS

CHAPTER ELEVEN

PART ONE

From The Eyes of Susan (Tutu) One of Mike's Best Friends.

Michael and I went through a lot together, hard times, good times, and some bad ones, but most of them were the best times of my life. I could write all day on the times that we had, but most of them are personal to me.

My best memories were with Michael. I'll share what I can. They might not be in order but I'll do my best.

When I first met Michael he was playing peewee football for Scottsburg with my cousin Shawn. He was standing in the parking lot at the Mary Bethune beside Tammy's car. Most of the fall and winter we only saw each other at the football games and at Shawn's house on Terry's Bridge Road.

By the time summer came, we were good friends. We'd all go fishing at the pond behind Shawn's house. We walked through the cow pasture and the woods. I remember one time we were all playing hide and seek in the dark and it was raining. He had on his camo and he was lying on the yard. I didn't see him lying there and of course, I lost. We all got sick and had the worst colds.

We went with Shawn to Richmond to the dentist, and he mooned a truck driver on the way. There were so many jokes. We laughed until we cried. There were many trips to Richmond and a lot of jokes and pranks.

We got really close. Then he started coming over to my house and we'd hang out, laugh, and talk. After that if we weren't staying at each other's house, we were talking on the phone and we'd talk for hours.

Most of our summers were filled with fishing and camping in my back yard. One time Michael and Shawn went fishing behind the dam in Halifax. I went with Rere (Shawn's mom) to pick them up, and they had caught this big catfish. He went to sling it in the van and smacked me right in the face with its tail. He laughed the whole way to Three Forks to weigh it. I was so mad at him. But now that I look back, it was so funny.

I remember the first time daddy heard Mike cuss. He was sitting on my couch and we didn't know that my Mama and Daddy were back from taking the trash out. Mike said something about ass and my daddy scared him so bad when he walked in the room and said, "You're not old enough to say ass, and if I hear you say it again I am going to whip your ass." I had never seen Mike move so fast in my life. It was so funny. We just laughed and laughed about that one.

Michael and I went and stayed at my sister's house on Mountain Road one night. The next day Shawn called Michael. He told Mike that he knew he had stayed with me and which couch we had sat on and where there had been a candle burning on the mantel. Mike's mouth fell open. It was so funny. We still have no idea how Shawn knew all that.

I stayed at Shawn's house one night with Mike and Shawn. Rere said that she had heard something outside. She thought she had seen someone next door. So Mike and Shawn got up and went to check it out. They came back and said they thought that it was someone in the house next door. They didn't think anything else about it. We all went back to bed. I was sleeping in the floor next to the window. A couple minutes after Mike turned out the light, I jerked the blind up, and scared the hell out of them. They jumped out of bed and turned the light on and I saw that they were white as a ghost.

I graduated in 2003. That was the summer that he flipped Jay's truck. When I climbed out, all we did was hold each other and cry all the way to talk to Jay.

One morning he woke up before I did, and he decided to wake me up by putting firecrackers in a metal bowl.

Michael was dating my cousin Maranda and they stayed at my house one weekend. Mike said he was going to take a shower but didn't move. I kept telling him to go take his shower, and he said I'm going. So I snuck in the bathroom and hid behind the shower curtain. He came in and shut the door, and locked it. Then he turned on the light. I jerked the shower curtain opened and said "Boo!" He grabbed me and had his fist drawn back. He said, "You're lucky I recognized your voice." We all laughed. But I never scared him again, that's for sure.

We went camping with Maranda during lake fest that year. The bathrooms were so far away from our campsite that I asked him to walk with me. Everyone else was asleep, but we couldn't sleep because it was so hot. We ended up walking around and talking for about three or four hours. He was so mad that he couldn't bring his fishing poles because of camp rules. He said that it was the only time that he had gone camping and couldn't fish. Michael and Maranda broke up around the fall of that year.

Then he started dating Amber and we all became friends. We all went to Amber's races together. By the time that Michael and Amber broke up we were the best of friends. We were closer than ever.

One of the times that I saw Michael cry was when no one could find Lil' Ronnie, his step-brother. He cried himself to sleep. He was worried that he would never see his brother again. I held him all night long and told him that everything would be okay. Later we found out that Lil' Ronnie was found and everything had worked out okay.

We stopped talking to each other one time for about three months. I don't even remember why now. It was the longest three months of my life. When he called, we picked up right where we had left off. Nothing had changed between us.

Mike, Shawn, and I went with my sister to Wal-Mart one night. We were walking around. Then we met back up with my sister at the bra and underwear section. We dared Mike to walk around Wal-Mart with a pair of green thongs on over his pants. He did, and we all busted out laughing. He walked around so proud with those things on.

Paula, Mike, and I were at my oldest sister's house by ourselves one day. Paula and I dared him to put on my sister's two-piece bathing suit. Well, of course he did and it was so funny seeing him strutting down the hallway.

When I got my driver's licenses I was babysitting for my aunt. I'd pick Mike up from school and we'd hang out. Then I'd take him home. Most afternoons after school Michael, Chell, Paula and I would play foosball over at Jay's. We all had a blast. It wasn't long before I started staying with him. Taking him and Chell to school and giving him a way back and forth to work.

One time Michael, Chell, and I went fishing at the Dan River and our friend Josh met us there. We fished for hours. Mike caught a big catfish. Then he decided to put it in a five-gallon bucket in the backseat with Chell on the way home. We were almost at Berry Hill Church when that fish almost jumped out of that bucket, and Chell almost jumped out the little window of the Beretta. Mike had to stop at the church because we were laughing so hard. He took his shirt off and put it over the bucket so Chell would get back in the car.

We would go riding through Falkland Farms late at night, then make a circle through Staution River State Park. We liked watching the albino deer grow up into a beautiful deer.

We met up with Lil' Ronnie, Devin and Emily fishing one night and it was so cold. But he wanted to stay, so I stayed with him. By the time he was ready to go I was a Popsicle. He thought I was joking. When we got home he skinned the fish and I took a hot shower. When he came in, I told him to feel my back. He did, and said, "Damn, Tutu. You were cold. I'm sorry." He held me close to keep me warm all night.

When his aunt Tammy came in from Florida I stayed at Lil' Ronnie's house because he was working out of town. Michael knew I didn't like being down there alone, so we came up with a plan. He would wait until everyone at his house was asleep, then he would sneak out of his bedroom window. Then I would pick him up at the end of his driveway so he could spend some time with me and I wouldn't be alone.

One day Penny and I were sitting on the swing at Jay's house. She was pregnant with JoJo at that time. Mike was playing horseshoes with Jay and Kenneth. Mike threw a horseshoe and it bounced off the box and hit me in the leg. I still have a hole where it hit me. Penny and I laughed at the fact that he didn't even stop playing long enough to check on me.

When I was babysitting for Penny and Kenneth, Mike dropped me off one morning. It was like five o'clock. He walked with me in the house, and then kissed me goodbye. He texted me a few minutes later and told me that he loved me, and that he would see me later.

I used to change his stuff around in his room a lot while he was at work. When he came home from work he would say, "Damn, Tutu! Did you get bored?" And then he just laughed.

He had some stinky feet. They smelled so bad. When I changed around in his room I wrote 'MF' on his side of the mattress. That way I'd know where his feet would be. I didn't want to smell his stinky feet while I was trying to sleep. When I told him what I did, he just laughed and looked at me and said, "Oh come on, Tutu. I thought you loved my feet."

We came home from Lil' Ronnie's one night and I had been drinking. I was pretty drunk. I had to go to the bathroom. Me, like a dummy, went in the bathroom, shut the door, locked it, and then turned on the light. When I turned around there was a black snake right at the toilet. It took me forever to get the door unlocked. I darted to the bedroom and told Mike that there was a snake in the bathroom! He said, "Sit down, Tutu. You're just drunk. Take a minute."

"NO!" I yelled. "THERE IS A SNAKE IN THE BATHROOM!"

He went and looked and said, "Damn! There is a snake." He yelled for Tammy. "Mama, where's the shovel? There's a snake in the bathroom."

The next day we told every body what had happened. Chell said the day before that Mike had seen the snake in the kitchen cabinet and was throwing everything out of the cabinet looking for it.

One time when we got back from Thanksgiving dinner at Nanny's we stopped by the house for a second. He was backing up to leave and backed right into Ronnie's big PMS work truck and busted the passenger side tail light out of my jeep. The next day he told Tammy that he backed into a tree while he was hunting because he didn't want to hear Ronnie fussing.

Mike, Chell, Paula and I would go riding all the time and I'd let Mike drive. My parents didn't really like me letting him drive because he wasn't on my insurance. So we would always switch at the end of my road. One night when Mike and I switched, Paula and Chell switched too. Mike and I looked at them like they were crazy.

Mike and I were riding one night on a back road. The car had an adjustable steering wheel. Out of nowhere Mike put the steering wheel all the way up, then stopped in the middle of the road. Then he said, "This is a school bus now. Get the hell out!" I looked at him. He had a sly smile on his face, clowning around, and we just laughed.

After Mike got his car I gathered everything that was mine and moved back home. We still spent a lot of time together.

Then he moved into his house and Paula and I went up there one night. He had drop cords running from Tammy's house because his power hadn't been turned on yet. We all had been drinking and I had to go to the bathroom. So we all walked to Tammy's house. He told us to be quiet and try not to make any noise. A few hours later, he was walking us back outside to the car and he fell over Jayden's walker. It took all we had to hold our laughter in until we got outside.

A couple months before Mike's passing, we spent a lot of time together. We went out to eat. We went pond fishing. I'd never caught anything in the ponds until I went with him.

He came to the cookout I had for my Mama for Mother's Day. He also stayed at my house the day I had my daddy's birthday party in May. That was the night we cried with each other. He said that he didn't want to lose me because he needed me. That he wanted to be with me. He told my Mama that he loved her and kissed her on the cheek. We had made plans for me to move in with him in July.

I helped him one day when he was working at Beth's. We were pulling weeds out of the flowerbeds. He looked at me, smiled and said, "Well, Doodle Nuts, let's move to the next one."

We also spent time with our friend Ashley. We were on the way to pick her up from her house one night and he hit a deer with my jeep. Then the next morning he hit another one on the same side of the jeep as the night before.

The Wednesday before he passed, we went fishing and had rented movies.

On Thursday I didn't go to work because I wanted to surprise him. When he walked in the door, he said, "I knew you didn't go to work, because I didn't see your jeep when I went by. I look to see if you're working every day I go by." And I just laughed. I took him to Wal-Mart that evening and he spent over 100 dollars in groceries.

That Friday I got up early. I took him to help a guy put some shingles on a roof. At about ten or so he called me to come pick him up. I pulled in the driveway and watched him take the big bundles up the ladder. I held my breath because it scared me so bad. He got in and looked at me and said, "What's wrong, Doodle Nuts? Was you scared I was going to fall?"

I said, "Yeah."

He said, "Don't worry about me. I'm going to be okay."

Later, he went with me to my house. While I was getting ready, he took a nap. Then took me to work that evening so he could keep my jeep. When it was time for me to get off work, he came back and picked me up. He cooked supper that night. Then he fixed my plate and something to drink and brought it to me. Then we fell asleep on the couch.

Saturday morning I was sitting on the couch and he was sitting beside me. Then he went to clean his tongue ring. He came running up the hallway and said, "Look, Tutu, at the hole."

I said, "Ew! I don't want to see that."

He went back to the bathroom and came back up the hallway and said, "So fresh and so clean, clean."

When I left him that morning to go home and get ready for work, he was sitting on the couch eating a bowl of cereal. I told him that I loved him and that I'd see him later.

He called me about three that afternoon. Then I talked to him again about seven. I asked him if they were having fun.

He said, "Yeah!" That he was waiting on me to get off and come down to Penny's. He added, "Call me when you get off. I'll see you later."

That was the last time we talked to each other. He's still here with me in my heart, and he checks in from time to time just to make sure I'm okay.

"Tutu"

Susan Hazelwood

Michael & his best friend Susan {Tutu}

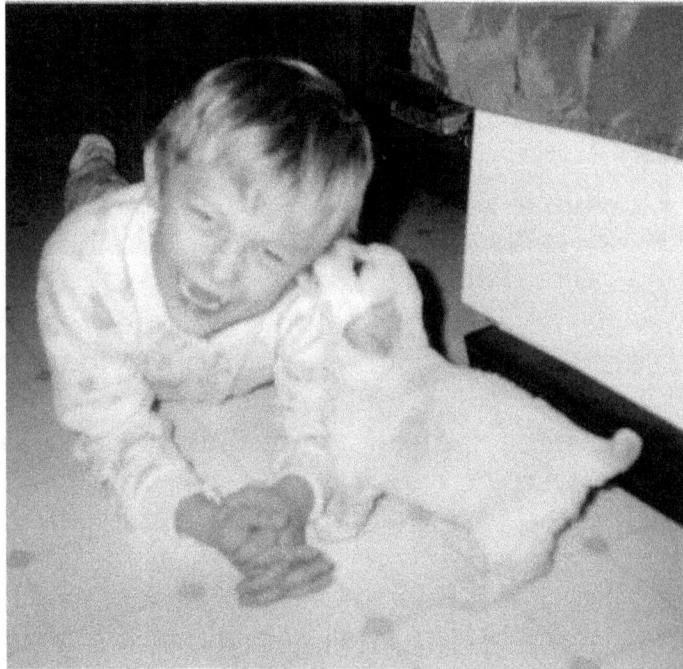

Michael playing with Nanny's dog, Fluffy

Michael holding Nanny's # 1 dog, Roo Roo

As you can see, Michael always loved dogs!
This is one of them, "Lil Pimpin", his # 1 dog.

Michael and his stepbrother "Lil Ronnie" in their favorite place, outside

Michael, Cousin DJ, Aunt Tammy, Cousin Mandy, Sister Michelle
with Scooter, From Jacksonville, Florida

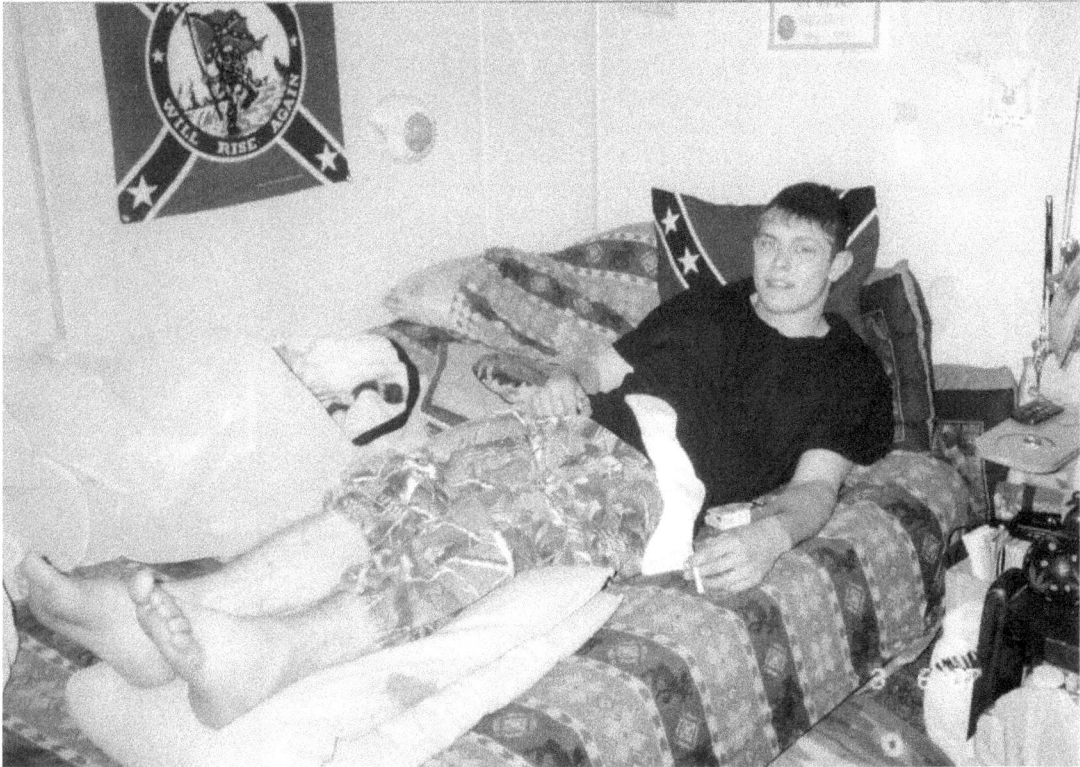

MICHAEL'S FAMOUS STINKY FEET

Here Michael has sprained his ankle and is showing off his stinky feet. Michael was also famous for breaking bones, after so many we lost count.

PART TWO

FROM THE EYES OF KITTY AND WADE SHORTT

PART TWO

FROM THE EYES OF KITTY AND WADE SHORTT

We live at 1051 Avondale Drive, Halifax Virginia. Avondale Drive runs parallel to highway 501 in the Centerville area. We purchased our home when our boys were young. We were close to Halifax and South Boston, but lived on a dirt road with little traffic. There are woods, streams, and trees, the whole country scene, or dreams come true in which to play. Wade and I both played in the woods when we were children and this place was just the perfect place to raise our boys.

One day Wade decided that the grandchildren needed a playground. So he had the lower lot cleared and cleaned out the creek. Then he built a "tree house" with a jail with bars under the tree house. He put a pole on one end of the tree house so that the children could make a fast escape. Then he and the grandsons designed and built a log cabin with a bridge over the creek. There's a tree just right for swinging across the creek, all this, and a tepee with a place to cook hot dogs. This is where our grandchildren and neighbor children would play all day when school was out. Kool-Aid was served on hot dog days, and sometimes cookies.

One summer morning when our grandson was visiting I was in the kitchen preparing breakfast and looked out of the window. That's when I saw two of the prettiest children I had ever seen, a little girl about five and a little boy about six or so with the most beautiful smile. I asked my grandson who those children belonged to. He replied, "Oh, they are our new friends. They stay with their grandmother Carolyn while their mother is working." Before the week was out, everyone in our house knew Michelle and Michael.

As Wade and I watched the children at play, we noticed that Michael was a leader. They rode bikes, played cowboys, designed play guns, and Wade would make those guns out of wood according to each child's personal design.

Time moved fast and the children wanted to "RIDE and DRIVE". Wade took a lawn mower and made it into a three seated "Dud-Mobile" with a place on the back to take trash to the local "green box." This was the boys' job and Michael took charge when the grandchildren were in Richmond. Wade wanted the children to learn how to drive, and he figured the Dud-Mobile was a good start. He always said, "We pay to teach our children how to swim. They would drive further in a lifetime than they would ever swim." He wanted them to know how to handle driving.

As Michael grew older he undertook the job of giving all the younger children a ride, and as they grew older he taught them how to drive. I have seen Michael ride the Dud-Mobile for hours. We never had to worry about him driving too fast or even reckless. Michael had a special way with the young as well as the adults.

I have seen as many as fifteen children in our back yard and never heard Michael raise his voice, whether it was playing cowboys or a game of basketball. He made sure that all bikes, balls and play things were put in their place and all trash picked up before the children called it a day.

Wade and I worried about Michael because he began to struggle and was losing interest in school. Wade taught Michael and Michelle to make some things using the equipment he had in his shop. Wade said that Michael just needed to know he could do whatever he set his mind to doing. He was right. Both of the children made some interesting things in Wade's shop.

Michael and Michelle were so special. I never heard Michael raise his voice or strike his sister or any other children playing in our yard. I was raised with three brothers and raised two sons and have three grandsons, so I know that getting into fusses with your brother or sister is part of growing up.

I think Michael taught me the meaning of what the Bible tells us in the book of Matthew Chapter five, verse nine: "God bless those who work for peace, for they will be called the children of God."Kitty & Wade said,

"What a BLESSING
To the Shortt Family
To have known
Michael Lee Johns!"

"I will always remember his big smile," they said.

Michelle and Michael in training for the Dud - Mobile!

Michael in his cowboy outfit
On his horse and ready to ride
to the Fort, Tepee, & Indians

Michael, friends, & Mr. Wilborn his principal, at Sinai Elementary School

Michael with just some of his awards from Sinai

Michael kept his big smile
It was his trademark!

CHAPTER TWELVE

FROM THE EYES OF TWILA & CEDRIC WALLACE

CHAPTER TWELVE

From The Eyes of Twila and Cedric Wallace

Michael, Cedric, and Michelle

I am Twila Wallace and this story is from my son Prince Cedric Wallace and me. I have a lot of good memories with Michael Lee Johns, some before Cedric was born and some after my son was born. But Michael and I, we go way back.

When I first met Michael, he was three years old. He was a typical little boy who loved splashing in mud puddles, carrying around his toy guns, playing Cowboys and Indians. Michael had a way about him that everyone loved. Yes, I was a sucker and came to love him and his family very much.

I started babysitting Michael and his sister Michelle all the time. I took Michael and Michelle pretty much everywhere I went. For quite some time, Michael didn't have teeth on top from a surgery he had to have. Only two teeth that made him look like a little vampire. I would pick on him and say, "Michael, you're my sweet and cute little vampire." Do you know what Michael's reply was?

Michael said, "I'm usually nice, but little vampires can be mean. But I'm not gonna eat blood!" For a moment there Michael thought he could be mean and tried to be a little vampire until he saw blood. Then he changed his mind. He didn't want to be a vampire any longer.

During the summer I would take Michael to the park. He loved the park because he could do pretty much anything. Michael's favorite thing at the park was the swings. He would say, "Push me high, Twila, so I can touch the trees."

Then I would get in the swing and Michael would sit in my lap facing me where we would swing together just laughing and having fun.

Michael also loved taking his cars and trucks to the park, because the park had hills that were always muddy. He would be at the top of the hill and I would be at the bottom, making noises and crashing them together, having a good old time.

When leaving the park, Michael would always thank me and say, "I love you so much. You're the only one who gets on the ground and plays cars and trucks in the mud with me and swings with me. When can we come back?"

As a child, Michael loved the game hide and seek. He and his sister Michelle were always asking please play hide and seek with us. Did I? Of course I did. I think they liked it so much because I would hide them in places that others usually wouldn't think of, like the dryer, refrigerator, freezer and clothes hamper. The joy I received was the look on their faces. It was priceless!

Through the years I took Michael many places, like the rodeo, the pool, and the fair, and we did many other things together. Michael really loved swimming, although he didn't want people to see his feet because he had two toes on each foot that were webbed together like his daddy. He was ashamed, but I told him that it just made him more special. I also said that I thought it was cool and that I wished I had toes like that. He finally overcame that issue, but one thing he never overcame was his stinking feet. His feet would smell up the whole house and then some.

I remember going to Michael's school functions. My son Cedric loved going to the school with me to get Michael and Michelle. Cedric would ask, "Mom, the next time we go to get Michael and Michelle from school, may I tell the office that I am here to pick them up?" I told him yes, and he was so excited. Then we went out in the hallway and wait for them. Here they came down the hall, and Cedric would run to them. Cedric and I loved them. Cedric thought of Michael as his very own brother, and I thought of him as my other son and called him that. We miss those days.

Michael Lee Johns also liked sports. He liked baseball and he played on teams. Michael and Michelle, I and my son Cedric were always playing baseball out in the yard. We all had a lot of fun. I taught Michael a whole lot about baseball. One of his baseball coaches asked him, who taught you how to play baseball? You are so good. Of course the coach said, your mom and dad? Then Michael said, "No, my second mama, Twila taught me."

Michael and his family lived on the farm, and in the woods behind the house just a little ways was a creek. Again Michael, Michelle, I and Cedric would go down there sometimes and play in the water. I remember this one time we were playing in the water, catching crawfish and sitting back on the rocks just enjoying ourselves. Not long after being there, the four of us had to pee. Well you know, the boys did their thing and Michelle and I did ours. Within a few minutes we decided to go down the creek a little ways and swing on the grapevines. As we started walking, Michael hollered, "Stop Cedric. Don't step there because that's where Twila and Michelle went to pee."

In turn we all stopped and asked, "Why, Michael?"

Michael replied, "If us boys step in girl's pee, then boys will get the cooties."

Michelle and I laughed so hard we cried. Don't you know that Michael and Cedric wouldn't step there either? We laughed even harder. As you can see, Michael Lee Johns was humorous.

Then there came the time when Michael and Michelle had to move to Georgia for a while because their mom got a job down there. My family and theirs were really upset about that. Those were the longest days and nights. Michael and Michelle really missed their family back home. They called every night and sometimes twice a day.

But it wasn't long before Michael called his Nanny Carolyn and said they wanted to move back to Virginia, and Mama wanted to move too. Can you come and help us? What sweet words. We jumped up and down for joy. You don't think we let Michael and Michelle down, do you? Hell no! We didn't. Nanny Carolyn, Cedric, myself, and their Aunt Penny couldn't pack fast enough and get out of Virginia. The faster we packed, the faster we could haul freight to Georgia.

Michael and Michelle were so happy to see us when we arrived. They couldn't stop smiling and hugging us. They were running around the house throwing their things in boxes. They were pushing and rushing their mama to hurry up and get their stuff packed. They were so afraid she would change her mind because of this guy she was interested in who lived there.

Well, we got the biggest U-Haul that you could get. It was like an eighteen wheeler. Papa Sammy had to work, so he had sent the money with us for the truck and gas. We were too impatient to wait for the weekend when he and Jay would be off work to go with us. We just had to get them out of Georgia and back in Virginia as quick as we could.

We were all packed up and the big truck was loaded down, along with Nanny Carolyn's truck, and ready to leave, we thought. Boy did we get fooled. The damn U-Haul was stuck right in the front yard. Fear set in! We sat, looked and thought a few minutes, and then decided us women can do anything with three kids. That's when all of us got the hoes and shovels, and started to dig it out. Then off we went. It was just too funny to be mad. We laughed at ourselves for awhile and made jokes, like who needs a man, surely not us independent women.

Heading back home laughing, singing, and out of Georgia, as quickly as possible, and guess what happened? We were just riding merrily down the interstate and suddenly a dead stop. Yeah! We got stuck in a traffic jam for two and a half hours.

After that we all decided to stop cracking jokes about needing men and started praising God. Once we got out of that mess, all of us started taking turns driving again. We were hoping to make up some of that time. Except for making as few potty stops as possible, we moved right along. Tammy, Michael, Michelle and Penny in the big U-Haul with Nanny Carolyn, Cedric, myself and two dogs loaded down to the gears in Nanny Carolyn's truck.

When we finally got back home to Virginia I remember Michael saying, "I'm so glad to be back home. Mama, you can move again if you want to, but I'm not ever leaving again." And Michael Lee Johns didn't, either!

As you can see, Michael loved his family. He was a family man. He really enjoyed all of his family gatherings, such as birthdays, holidays, Easter egg hunts, fishing trips, vacations, and reunions, and to my knowledge, he never missed any of them. When he got too old to hunt the eggs, then he came and helped hide them for the younger kids.

Michael Lee Johns was very talented with his hands also. He was a great artist. He loved to draw and was excellent at it. My son Cedric was always after Michael to draw with him. Michael took a lot of time with Cedric, and Cedric treasures those memories. Michael was also great at making woodworks and lots of crafts, too many to name them all. He made birdhouses for his Nanny Carolyn. Magazine racks and remote control holders, walking canes, and more, and gave all those to his family as well. Michael was just a very gifted and special young man. I always called him by his whole name. He loved that, too.

Michael had other hobbies he loved, and one of them was hunting. I can't shed any light on that subject because I didn't care a thing about hunting. Although I do know he went hunting with his Uncle Jay and Papa Creasy a lot, and over the years Michael killed many deer.

Guess what else Michael loved to do in his free time? He loved fishing. Michael, his sister Michelle, I and my son Cedric went fishing quite often. Michael was a real fisherman. He taught Michelle, Cedric and I how to fish. The three of us didn't know how to bait the hook, or how to cast the line in the water, or even how to take the fish off once we caught it. We wouldn't skin the fish either, and had no idea as to how to clean them or cook them. Michael did all that for us and never complained for a long time. Then one day Michael realized that he wasn't really getting any fishing time for himself. So eventually he said, "Something needs to change here. You know I like to fish, too."

So do you want to know what happened after that day? We learned how to do it ourselves, but it took a little while.

I remember going fishing one time and the four of us caught thirty-two fish within three hours. So like I said, Michael was a fisherman and he taught us all how to catch fish. Shortly afterward, we stopped that day and went back to the cabin. Michael couldn't teach us how to clean the fish because we refused to learn how, so Michael had all those fish to clean. About half way through the cleaning process he said, "No more fishing today. I taught y'all too well!"

Later Michael came in the cabin, washed them one last time and cooked them. We ate that night until we were all running over. They were so good. How blessed were we to have Michael?

I remember sometimes we would make a bet as to who would catch the most fish. Usually it was it the boys, but Michelle and I snuck a few in on them. Oh, how I miss those days. There's not a time that I go fishing now that I don't think about those days with Michael, and neither does Cedric.

We loved going to the lake. Michael, Michelle, Cedric and I would go to the lake as often as we could. We would swim, go boat riding, fish, and have picnics. No matter what we did, we always had fun together. Michael loved water skiing and inner tubing. Cedric and Michelle did too, but they weren't as good at it as Michael. Cedric would beg Michael to please ride the inner tube with him, and Michael always did. I'm glad Cedric has lots of memories of Michael, and they are all good memories, fun times with him.

Let me tell you that here in Virginia we have an event that's called a Mud Bog or Mud Slinging. This is where big 4x4 trucks and fired-up big cars race in the mud. Some of the vehicles get stuck every time; altogether, most of them would get through. We would have to wear old clothes when we went because they threw mud everywhere. Michael always wanted to go to the Mud Bog. He loved it.

When we left the Mud Bog, we would have mud from our heads to our toes. Mud all in our hair, face, neck, clothes, and shoes, everywhere was mud. People would see us driving back to the house and knew where we were coming from and laughed along with us. Ah, to be covered in mud was right up Michael's alley. One time we were driving back to the house and Michael said, "I want to get me a big truck like that so I can drive in the Mud Bog. After I get my truck, you, Cedric and Michelle can ride in it with me." That never happened here on this earth, but one day in heaven it will, Michael.

Michael spent a lot of days and night with us, and we really enjoyed each other's company. He didn't have to go places to have fun. He was just as satisfied and happy sitting around the house with us, playing cards and watching T.V. Michael loved playing his favorite game, a dice game called Faukle. He was so lucky at that game. He would say, "I should go to Las Vegas, because I can win a lot of money." The thought of that always made his face light up like a Christmas tree.

Here's the icing on the cake! How many eighteen-year-olds do you know that had their own place to live in? A job and a vehicle? Not too many, I tell you, but Michael Lee Johns did. He was proud of himself and his accomplishments. He paid his own mortgage, taxes and insurance. Yes he struggled, and at times it was hard, but he was determined to do it. He didn't want his family to support him, especially his Nanny Carolyn. Michael accepted responsibility like a man when he stepped up to bat, a real champ! He paid his way. He didn't like the freeloaders, he called them, especially those that took advantage of his Nanny Carolyn. He didn't believe freebies were right. Do you want to know the real kicker? Michael Lee Johns also kept a very clean house. As long as I've known Michael, he was very wise, and I remember him saying, "If you pay your own way, then you will take better care of your stuff and respect it more."

I believe Michael marked my son Prince Cedric Wallace. The reasoning behind that belief is Cedric favors and looks like Michael a whole lot, when Michael was the age Cedric is now. Cedric is also outspoken like Michael. The mixture of Cedric's blonde and brown hair, blue eyes, the build of his body at this time, the things he says, and just all around his whole demeanor reminds me so much of Michael daily. Michael thought the world of Cedric and treated him like he was his own brother. The closeness between them is something that Cedric will cherish for the rest of his life. I guess you could say in a way Michael really is like my firstborn son. I don't think I or Cedric could have loved him any more if he had been. He was just so easy to love.

Then I remember the last time that Cedric and I saw him in his physical body. It was 2008 at the Ducks On The Dan. As always, we all had a grand old time. We laughed, shared various memories and told jokes. The last thing Michael said to me was, "I'll call and see you in a few days so you can fix me those shrimp tostados. I like them so much." Smiling with a big grin, he said, "Bye and love you."

I replied back at him, "Okay! We'll have to do that. Love you back." He smiled, waving at us as he walked out of our sight.

The last call that I got wasn't from Michael, but his Nanny Carolyn. She told me that Michael had been shot and died. My heart dropped to my feet. My life was turned upside down for a long while. I felt so sad and so lost. I wish I could have had one last time to tell Michael that I loved him.

Over a period of time, I finally found peace again. What did I do to get my peace back? I remembered all our good times together. I shared with anyone that would listen about our good times. And I finally convinced myself that Michael Lee Johns was just another angel in heaven looking down over us, to protect Cedric my son and myself.

As you can see, Michael was a very well-rounded young man. He was fearless. He loved and lived life to the fullest. Many people live fifty years or more and never find the joy and life Michael Lee Johns had his whole life on earth. He loved life and his family and friends. He was secure and confident. He knew who he was and where he was going, and what he wanted out of life. Michael didn't know any strangers. He loved people, everyone. Michael was loving, caring, respectful, kind, compassionate, always willing to lend a helping hand to anyone. He was very outspoken and didn't mind speaking up when he saw someone bullying another person. That was his character, his nature. He had all the goodness and it all just came to him.

Michael, you were my other son, my best friend and someone whom I will always cherish and keep close in my heart! So, Michael Lee Johns, I will end with this:

Michael, Oh Michael, we miss you. Michael, Oh Michael, we really do.

Michael, Oh Michael, I love you so much. Michael, I wish you were here so I could feel your touch. Michael, Oh Michael, God knew best when he called you home, Michael, and laid you to rest. Michael, do something for me and tell my grandma Arrington and Papa Watts "hi". While family and friends still try to understand why. Michael, Oh Michael, you see the pain inside of my heart. But Michael I know you're not so far away. We really aren't apart. Michael, you send us many memories of your undying love. Michael, I bet you're watching the doves up above. Michael, so for now we will have to wait. Michael, Oh Michael, until it's our time and you meet us at heaven's gate."

"I LOVE YOU MICHAEL LEE JOHNS"

Love from Twila & Cedric!

Cedric Wallace

Michael Lee Johns

Michael loved boats and sailing!

Michael, I miss your ball games!

Show them your fists, Michael and Michelle!
Don't Mess With My Sister!

Look at Michael's attitude and Chell's big smile!
They decided to switch!

My Little Vampire!

Now that's my muddy boy!
Another Look-A-Like! I do believe he marked my son Cedric!

Outdoors, my 2nd home!

Michael's Mud Bog Truck!
Where's The Mud Bog?

CHAPTER THIRTEEN

THE LAST CONVERSATIONS

Michael, Christmas 2007
When his Nana cried, a death in family or she was ill he would say,
"Nana, you can't die as long as I live
My heart can't live without you.
So please stop crying?
And give me a SMILE."
Then with a big hug,
Squeezing her ever so tight,
Kissed her on her forehead and say,
"I Love You, Nanny"!

CHAPTER THIRTEEN

THE LAST CONVERSATIONS

It was June 21st 2008, Saturday, and Penny and Kenneth were having a cookout in honor of their son JoJo, who was stillborn June 17th 2005. Sam and I were attending the Phillips's family reunion instead of going to the cookout. We had planned to run up to the farm later that evening, if we weren't too tired.

Around noon, Michael called. "Nana, are you and Papa coming up for the cookout? Kenneth said you weren't coming."

I explained it was the five-year reunion and Papa had some family members that he only got to see at those reunions from out of state.

He said, "Okay, Nana, I will see you later then. I love you." And he hung up.

But a few minutes later the phone rang again and it was Michael. "Nana, are you sure you aren't coming up to the cookout? I need to talk to you."

I replied, "Michael, what is it, son? If it's that important, we will come. We can miss the Phillips reunion. What do you want to talk to me about? Can you tell Nana now?" Michael didn't sound worried, but almost afraid.

Michael said, "Nanny, you know my girlfriend has been staying here with me sometimes. But I'm going to move her stuff back to the gashouse tonight or in the morning. Nanny, remember when I came down and told you about her throwing fits, hitting and kicking me? She acts like some crazy person sometimes. I love her, but I can't live like that. All she wants to do is fight and hit. I can't do anything to please her. So we decided it would be best for her to move out and go on to college. Maybe when she finishes college, we can get along and try it again. Nanny, I don't know what she might pull."

I said, "Michael, what do you do when she is slapping and kicking you? You don't hit her, do you? Are you afraid of her or afraid she or her family might hurt you?"

"No, Nana! But she tells her family I hit her. But I don't. I swear, Nana, I have never hit her. Everything she does to me, she tells them I do to her. She lies so bad, Nana. I want to hit her sometimes, but I don't. I just walk away and that makes her crazy. Then she throws stuff at me. I wish I never taught her how to use the rifle. But I swear to God, Nana, I have never touched her. She even says she will kill me if I break up with her. But Nana, I can't take any more."

I jumped in. "Michael, are you afraid of her? What kind of stuff has she thrown at you? Has she ever pointed a gun at you? When? Do you think she would shoot you? Michael, you need to get away from her and her family as fast as you can. Yes, Papa and I will come up there. Forget about the reunion."

"No, Nana, I'm not afraid of her." He was laughing at me. "Don't get upset, Nanny. I told her if she ever hurt me she would have to deal with you and Papa. She is all mouth. She threatens to shoot me. But I tell her to go ahead. I'm not afraid of her or death. Then she calms down and then she's sorry. She throws whatever she can get her hands on at me, knives, shoes, just stuff, Nanny. But that's why she's moving out for good. She won't work and help me with bills. Every time she says she's getting a job, she claims she has some kind of anxiety attack, but there's nothing wrong with her when she does nothing all day but sit and talk on the phone. She won't cook or clean. Nanny, some days she won't even get dressed until I get here. She is just so negative and she speaks so badly about everybody. All the time, Nanny, she never has anything good to say. She thinks her looks will get her anything she wants out of life and her sex. " He laughs again.

I said, "Well, what does she do all day while you are at work?"

Michael answered, "Talks on the phone and carves my name on bullets. She says she's gonna kill me, Nanny. She thinks about that all the time when I'm at work. She says she wants to know what it feels like to kill someone."

I said, "Michael, she is crazy. Get her out of your house and life. You know Papa and me will help you. Don't worry about the mortgage. Just get her off that farm."

"Nana, there's something else, and I hope you'll be okay with it. Tutu, you know Susan, my best friend. She is moving in tonight when she gets off work. She will come here around 10:30 tonight and spend the night. Then we will pack up the rest of (girlfriend's) things and move her in the morning. Tutu works and will help me with the bills. You and Papa have done enough for Chell and me. She is my best friend and I can count on her doing her half. Is that okay with you?"

I said, "Michael, how does (girlfriend) feel about that? That would make me crazy mad if I knew you were moving me out and moving in another girl. I don't care if Tutu moves in. But you know girls don't like to be replaced, even by a best friend. Does (girlfriend) know she's moving in tonight?"

Michael laughed and said, "Yeah, Nana. It's not like that. She's okay with it. Besides, she's going to VA Tech this fall and she will probably meet someone up there. And I don't care if she does. I just need her to move out of my house. You don't understand, Nana. When she drinks, she's crazy. But when she's sober, she is nice. She's just got to go because she won't work and when she drinks she hits me, kicks me, and threatens to shoot me." Then he laughs again and adds, "I just wish I never taught her how to shoot that rifle."

"Okay, Michael, so you don't need us to come up there and help you, is that right? You be careful. If we aren't too tired when we get back from the reunion, we'll ride up anyway. Call me on my cell if you need me to come before then okay."

Michael laughed and said, "Naw, Nana, you don't need to come up here. As long as you're okay with Tutu moving in tonight, and (girlfriend) getting out. I don't need you to come up. I will come by there tomorrow to see you and Papa. I love you, Nana." Then he hung up.

That was the last conversation I had with Michael in his physical body. Sam and I went on to the reunion and returned home around 5 pm. Since Michael hadn't called, we decided to lie down and rest an hour, and then ride up. But we both were more tired than we realized. It was 8 pm when we woke up. I jumped up. I called Penny to see if the crowd was still there and to say we weren't coming. No one answered, so we decided they were out in the pool and would call us back.

Around 9 pm our phone rang and Penny screamed in the phone, "Mama, get up here to the farm. Michael has been shot."

Shocked, I said, "Shot? When? Where?"

She said, "Just get up here Mama. I think Michael is dead." Then she hung up.

I ran to the bedroom screaming for Sam to get up. "Michael has been shot. Get up. We've got to go to the farm." We ran out the door and drove the longest five miles we have ever driven in our life. I didn't think we would ever get there. Praying all the way, "Lord please, please don't let him be dead. Lord please, please let Michael live. Lord, you raised Lazarus. If Michael is dead, you've got to raise him up. Please Lord, I am begging you. Please don't let my baby be dead."

Sam tried all he could to stay calm, but he couldn't hold back the fear and tears either. He said, "Maybe they were just playing around and the gun went off and Penny just panicked."

But as we got near Michael's driveway, we saw all the police cars and rescue lights and crowd of people. I drove up as close to the door as I could. I noticed there was no yellow ribbon around the house, and commented that to Sammy.

He said, "See, maybe it's just an accident and Michael is alright. Otherwise there would be yellow tape."

I jumped out of the car and ran in the house, Sammy right behind me. Jay tried to grab and stop me when Penny grabbed me and pulling me back screaming, "Stop her. Stop, Mama. Don't let her go in there. She has a heart problem."

I screamed at them as I pulled away and said, "Michael is my heart. Turn me loose. Turn me loose. That's my grandson in there. You won't stop me from seeing him."

I ran through Michael's front door and right past the cop and down the hall before anyone could get their hands on me. As I approached his bedroom door I saw Michael lying on the floor in the doorway. I dropped to my knees and screamed, "Oh, Michael. Michael. What happened? No Michael, tell me she didn't do this! You told us, and we didn't listen. Michael, my baby, my son. "

Then suddenly I felt a presence to my right and looked up. I immediately saw Christ and Michael standing over the body in all light. Michael was scratching his head and said, "Dang, she actually did it, Nanny. I didn't think she would. But she actually shot me. I just laid there and let her, Nanny. I just laid there because I didn't think she would. She was drunk. But I didn't think she was that drunk."

I just sat on my knees at his lifeless head staring up, and listened to Michael with Christ standing there at his feet looking down over the body. I couldn't believe what I was seeing, and especially what I was hearing.

Suddenly someone yelled, "No, Nanny. Don't touch him." As soon as they yelled Michael and Christ vanished. (Someone later said it was Tim Conner.) Then he and Jay pulled me up from the floor while I screamed, "Turn me loose, turn me loose, you don't understand."

But they kept right on dragging me up that hall. About midway I noticed a fist hole to my right on the wall. Jay said, "No, Mama. I did that. When I came in and saw Michael lying there, I got mad and hit the wall. I will fix it."

I suddenly pulled myself together when I smelled alcohol on Jay's breath. Then I said very authoritative, "Leave me alone! Turn me loose!" As I pushed my elbow back from his arm hold, and continued, "Just let me sit on the sofa." Then I noticed the girlfriend's clothes lying at the end of the sofa and asked, "Where is (girlfriend)?" But they overpowered me and led me outside on the porch instead.

I asked where was Tammy and Michelle? Someone said they had been called. Then I turned and said I needed to sit down. My legs were shaking so bad, I knew I would fall. I asked Sam to find my shoe that I had lost from our car to the porch, as I walked in the house and sat on the sofa. By that time Jay had walked on away from me and over to a car.

As soon as I sat down on that sofa, calmness came over me. I looked down the hall to see if I could see Michael and Christ in all light again. Instead I saw Michael's body lying on the floor, but I knew they were there, just behind that door, hovering over the body. Then I noticed the whole house was filled with a peace that only God could make happen. I saw the officer standing at the door. I saw Penny and Sam sitting in the living room with me.

I immediately asked if anyone had called Kristi. Penny replied she would, and used my phone to call her. After that I just sat on that sofa where I could see Michael's body, the officer, the front door and Jay coming through and going out. I could see other people as they watched me and waited. I heard someone say that the girlfriend never called for help. That the neighbor was outside in their yard having a birthday party also, and that's why Tim was there to start with. Then I heard someone say she ran away naked, but the cops caught her and made her put on some clothes. I just sat and listened and watched down the hall for a flash or a glance of Christ and Michael in all light again, just one more time, I thought to myself.

After two hours or more, someone said the coroner was coming. I sat and watched him walk through with his bag straight to Michael's body.

About thirty minutes later, someone said the investigating officer had arrived. I stood up and went to the door where I could watch him and see what he did first. Why? I don't know. I just felt a push, like someone was pushing me up off the sofa and to the door. I saw him look to his right to a car sitting near his, and at a lady standing inside the car holding on to the car door, and I saw another person sitting in the passenger side front seat. Then I saw them make eye contact and nod heads at each other like they were saying everything was going to be alright.

Then he turned and walked toward the porch and stepped inside. He first looked around and then apologized for being so late. He smiled and said he had been to a party in Riverdale for him and his fiancé. Then he walked straight back and looked at the body. He laughed and stated to the coroner who was still back there taking pictures that it looked like a suicide to him. When he looked up the hall and saw me watching him, he tried to shut the door. But Michael's body was in the way, so he said help me turn him, and then he pushed the door up but not closed. I could hear him laughing and a little talk, but couldn't make out what they were saying.

Within five minutes the investigator walked up the hall in a hurry and asked where his mother was. That's when I stood up and followed him out as Penny or someone told him she was outside. I followed him over to Tammy and in turn he asked her to step inside his vehicle. He said he was sorry for our loss. That there must have been one hell of a fight in there, and whatever they were fighting over, your son just decided to end it. I spoke up and said, "You determined all that in just five minutes." The investigator turned to the back seat and asked who I was. Tammy said I was her mother. Then he said, "Yes, Madam. I have determined it as a self-inflicted wound." On that note, I got out of his truck and went back inside the home, sat down and waited for the coroner.

The coroner took a few more pictures and then he came up the hall. He got to the front door and turned and said he was sorry for our loss.

I asked him if he thought it was a suicide.

He looked straight at me with shock on his face, like I had asked a confused question, and said, No. He wasn't making that call. He was sending the body to Richmond for a second autopsy. No, he said again, he wouldn't make that call and again said, he was so sorry for our loss. Then he asked if I would like to leave before they put him in a body bag and carried him out.

I replied, "No. You are not putting him in a body bag. Only his body. I have sat here for over three hours and saw my grandson's body lie on that floor. I will sit here until they carry his body out of this house. Then I will leave. "

He answered alright then, and thanked me for correcting him and turned and walked out of the door. That was the last time I saw and spoke with that coroner.

A few minutes later the EMTs came in and bagged his body as I watched them. Then they carried his body out of his home. The place he loved so much. The last place his flesh body would be on that farm alive.

I followed his body out, and when I reached the bottom of his steps I turned and walked over to Tammy and Michelle standing outside crying. Tammy and Michelle had cried so long and so hard, their faces looked funny. The look on their face was disbelief, confusion, and how could God allow this? They couldn't believe what they were witnessing, Michael's body dead. When just a few hours earlier they were all eating and laughing together. Now they stood and watched them leave Michael's driveway with Michael's body, as the cops got in their cars one by one and left behind them.

Finally the investigator spoke with the girlfriend, the only person with Michael at the time of his physical death. The only person who was screaming she didn't mean to in her naked self. The only person screaming ugly things about Michael in his yard while everyone else grieved, and the only person besides the investigator that said he killed himself.

After the investigator got in his vehicle to leave, I walked down to the girlfriend and asked her what happened there that night. She looked up at me and answered in front of her mama, "It was an accident, Nanny. I didn't mean to do it. I swear, Nanny." Then I saw her mama tap her on her right shoulder and the girlfriend went to telling me some story that didn't even make sense. But as she looked at her mama, I felt the mama was controlling that situation, so I just walked away. I then walked over to Tammy. She asked if I was coming over to her house.

I replied, "No, I need to go home and pray. I need some answers. Michael has left the farm, so I will too. I don't want to see or talk to anyone else tonight. I don't want to hear any more. My grandson has left his body and I need God to tell me or show me why." With tears flooding down my face and my body shaking so bad I could barely put one foot in front of the other, I reached over and hugged her. Then I proceeded to my car and got in. Sammy had been standing over next to Chuck, and when he saw me he followed. And we left the farm.

Driving out on Old Mill Road was lonely. Just thinking a few moments earlier my grandson's body was in a bag on its way to Richmond. Then I turned to Sammy and said, "We should have come up here to that cookout today. We knew Michael was concerned for his life. That's why he called us and asked us to come up today. Michael has never called us before and asked if we were coming up to a cookout. But we had never missed one before, either. We're smart people, Sammy, we should have read between the lines and came up today. Then there wouldn't have been any drinking. When did they start drinking at cookouts, anyway? They have never drank before."

Sammy answered, "We didn't know. We didn't know that Kenneth would even have any alcohol there. I thought he didn't drink. Maybe she brought it with her. Michael said she was a crazy bitch, but I don't think she's that crazy. Of all the places, I thought Michael was safe at Penny's at the cookout with family. Well, we didn't know they would be drinking either. What else is there that we don't know about?"

I answered, "I don't know, but I will get the answers. What Michael told me today keeps going over in my head. That everything she does, she turns it around and tells her family and friends that he's doing it to her. You know Michael has never gotten in trouble for fighting in school or anywhere else. Except that one time she talked him into a fight with some guy over her. But Michael learned his lesson and told her she would never get him in trouble again. Besides, that was a guy, anyway. Michael would never hit a girl. We used to tell him to hit Michelle, and maybe she would leave him alone. But he never would." We both laughed at that memory. Silence filled the car the rest of the way home.

My heart hurt to the bone. My body shook. We drove up in the driveway and I said, "You know, the farm will never be the same again. All the money and time we have spent on that farm was for the grandchildren. We never wanted it or wanted to live there. Michael loved that farm. Now that Michael is gone, I don't know if any of the others will love and care for it or not."

Sam turned the motor off and we just sat there a minute like we both were hoping it was all a bad dream. I noticed Sam was holding his chest, and I gathered enough strength to ask if he was alright. He replied he would be just as soon as they arrested that bitch for killing Michael. Then he reached for the door handle and opened the door, and turned back and asked if I could get out and walk in the house. I opened my door and got out and followed him in the house. Sammy never stopped. He went straight to the bedroom. He never liked to show emotions around people. So I knew he had gone to be alone to cry, to get some of that pressure off his chest.

I walked over to my chair to sit down and noticed it was 1:20 a.m. I turned and looked for Mercy, our little blind Chihuahua, who sat in the chair, to make sure I didn't sit on her. When I bent to sit and as I turned back around, I felt a strong presence and looked up. There Michael stood in my den floor in all light, with his arms outstretched. "Nana, I didn't do this. But it's all right. Its God's doings. I am not dead. See, Nana?"

I sat down crying out, "Oh Michael. Michael? What happened? No, it's never going to be alright. I can't touch you, hug you and kiss you. It's never going to be alright. Why, Michael? Why did you just lie there and let her shoot you?"

Then again he said, "Nanny, (that's what he called me when he wanted something), I didn't do this." Then I felt him sit beside me on my right side in the chair. I felt him place his left arm around me as his right hand wiped the tears from my eyes. Then he whispered in my right ear as I felt his breath with each word. "Nanny, don't cry. Please don't cry. You will. You will see me. You will hear me. Nanny, you will feel me. Its okay, Nanny. It's God's doings. You will and you will understand. I love you, Nanny. Please don't cry." Then I felt him just vanish.

I sat there a few more minutes and tried to stop crying, but thoughts kept filling my mind. How could it be God's will to give us Michael and then take him from us so soon? Nineteen, Lord. He was just nineteen.

"He was twenty to the day," I heard a voice say. I stopped and listened for more, but that was all the voice said.

The archangel announced your birth, Michael, and I saw you before you were ever formed in your mama's belly. I saw your mama in hard labor as she was willing to give up her life so you could live. I watched it all like I was watching television on a big flat screen. Then I lived to see you be born and come forth. I lived to see you move to Virginia like the Archangel Gabriel said you would. But nothing, I got nothing from you, Lord, to prepare me for this day. You showed me nothing about his death. Are you just going to leave us with unanswered questions, Lord? Now I have to live out my days without Michael. Then I laughed. I realized I was laughing. After awhile I said out loud, "Well, Michael, as much as you loved guns, it was the perfect way for you to leave your body." But no sooner than I heard my own words out loud, the laughter turned back to tears.

I knew it was my selfishness that wanted him in his body. I knew he couldn't have passed from his body unless it was God's will. But it just didn't make any sense at all to me. I thought about my nephew, Lil' Tommy, who would have been eighteen years old on his birthday if he had just lived one stinking month longer. I thought about his birth and life, and how he shined for God. The young and the old loved him with a passion, just like Michael. I asked God, you are our Father, why do you give us the children of light and then allow them to die physically before they turn twenty-one? You have blessed my immediate family with two of the light children, and we haven't gotten to enjoy their lives to twenty-one. I don't understand. Please help me to understand. I need your strength and wisdom right now.

Then I remembered our phone conversation earlier that day. I knew he wasn't afraid of death or anyone. What happened, Michael? What happened, God? Please give me some answers. Show us some proof, something as to why this happened. With every thought 'that it was alright' just made me hurt and cry even more. Michael's own words, "Nana, I didn't do this. But it's alright. It's God's doings." Those words rang in my ears like a church bell, and with every ding my bones hurt with grief. How can it ever be alright to be shot in your own home for no reason but rage and jealousy, I screamed out?

I wanted to hit the walls. I wanted to hit them so hard that every picture that hung on them fell and broke. I wanted my heart to just stop beating. But instead, I just sat and cried until there were no more tears. Then I just sat in the silence with my eyes closed. Like at the farm, my mind was still. Not one thought flowed through it. Just that still silence in the secret place with God. I could feel God bathing me in his love like cool, warm water flowing over me. I could feel the beauty of this room I had entered. I just sat with my eyes closed and let God rub my body like a loving husband would rub lotion on his beautiful wife's body. With each of Jesus's hands I felt the healing balm flow through me. How long I stayed in this silence, I don't know.

Suddenly like I woke up and knew that calmness that had filled his house earlier filled the whole room. I knew I was in the presence of a great being, even though I couldn't see it. I felt a body sitting next to me ever so gently and tenderly on my right side. I felt his arms wrap around me. I felt him squeeze me tight as he lifted me up out of the chair. Then I felt him walking me to the daybed and ever so gently laid me down. I felt him as he reached for the covers and covered me, clothes and all. Then I felt his hand push back my hair as he leaned over me and kissed me on the forehead. Like a fast-acting sleeping pill had kicked in, I dropped off to sleep or in a trance.

I slept until morning. A very peaceful and restful sleep. I really thought it was just a bad nightmare, a bad dream, so I jumped up to call Michael. When I jumped up, I felt it. It wasn't just a bad dream. It was real, wasn't it, Lord? It was real! My beautiful baby boy with his heavenly smile was smiling in heaven with Jesus now.

That was the last conversation I had with Michael, and the last time I felt him for several days. Christ's peace and calmness remained during those days. I noticed that I couldn't hang around negative energy very long and would get up and walk outside and sit alone.

When I did share a little, before I just clammed up about it altogether, here are a few of the comments I heard from some people. Some people called it shock; they said I was in shock. Others said my mind was playing tricks on me. Still others said, and this is a good old fashioned answer, your nerves can play all sorts of games with you.

I laughed at their ignorance. For I knew of no one in a mental hospital or that had a nervous breakdown had ever experienced what I had the night before. It was ignorance many years ago that put my Aunt Ruby in the Lynchburg Training Center for testifying that God talked to her. The same people my daddy and my Aunt Ellen protected me from as a child, and let me add, some well-meaning preachers were among that group. Those memories just clammed my mouth shut tight as tight-fitting jeans, as Conway use to say. And I refused to tell anyone what our Lord Jesus Christ or Michael had allowed me to experience the night before for many days after. When someone made such an ignorant comment to me, I smiled at them and remembered what Saint Paul said in the Bible, "If they choose to be ignorant, then so be it."

June 22nd. Half the morning was gone and all I had done was sit, drink coffee and smoke little cigars. My brother Tommy called. He said they were in town and on their way over. I was glad because he and his lovely wife Carol believe in the supernatural, and I knew I needed to stay surrounded by people of light. They knew I had walked with their son in the supernatural for ten months during his illness. I was there with Lil' Tommy when he crossed over, and then walked with him after he left his body as he taught me about heavenly things. I knew they would understand or just keep silent.

Then my brother James called. He said he and Joan were on their way. I mustered up enough air to say okay. He was another family member who believed in the supernatural, one whom I sat with for days in and days out during the weeks and months and years, just talking about spiritual things together. I said okay but just sat in my chair. I made no attempt to get dressed or comb my hair or anything. I just sat and drank coffee and smoked those little cigars. I couldn't talk. Every time I tried, all I did was cry. Later my baby sister Joyce called. She said she was bringing Aunt Elsie and would meet us at Tammy's. Then she said, Okay, sis? I said okay but I just sat.

Around noon the phone rang and it was my sister Joyce again. She said, "Meet me at Tammy's. Aunt Elsie is with me, okay sis? Say you are coming to Tammy's."

For some reason her voice woke me up and I jumped up and said we have to go to Tammy's. Tommy jumped up and said okay. Carol asked if I wanted to bathe and change clothes. My answer shocked her when I shouted.

"NO. I HAVE TO KEEP THESE CLOTHES ON. MICHAEL TOUCHED THESE CLOTHES AFTER HE STEPPED OUT OF HIS BODY. DIDN'T I TELL YOU?"

Carol replied, "No. Tell us. You've seem him, haven't you? I told Tommy I bet Michael had come to you." So my mouth flew open and I shared the spiritual experience on the way to the farm, with the same clothes on.

As we turned off Grubby Road, Tommy noticed all the deer standing on the roadside and said, "Look. Look at the parade of deer. I've never seen anything like it. They're lined up both sides of the road. Look, Carolyn. Do you see them? They are standing at attention as we pass by."

I yelled, "Yes, I see them. They do. Don't they? Have you ever seen such a beautiful sight?"

Tommy said again, "Look. I have never seem anything like this."

Carol said, "Look! They are honoring you, Carolyn. They know you're Michael's grandmother. They are honoring you. Have you ever?"

We watched the deer as we passed by just stand on the side of the road like soldiers. The most beautiful sight we had ever seen. Some just stood and watched us pass. Others nodded their heads like they were bowing to us. Yet others just stood so still as if they were statues. All the way to Michael's house, deer were lined up on both sides of the road. From Grubby Road to Union Church Road to Old Mill Road they stood. Hundreds, I wanted to say thousands of them, since there were so many. At least five miles long they stood at attention. It did feel like they were honoring us as we passed through.

I said, "It's like they know the earth has lost a great and precious gift. Like they know one of God's most precious light children has left the earth realm."

When we got to Tammy's we shared the deer parade. Many made comments about them being Michael's deer. All the deer he shot while in his earth suit. They laughed and joked about it, enjoying the happy memories. It felt good to have lifted everyone's spirits, even if it was just for a few moments. Everyone that knew Michael knew he could out-hunt them all. Some said they believed Michael just stood in the woods and called the deer to come to him so he could shoot them. Others said it was Michael just letting us know he was still with us. Just being there at Tammy's and hearing all those comments made me feel better. To hear them say what I had thought but hadn't said. So I just made a smile to push back the tears.

The rest of the week we had funeral plans to make while we waited for his body to be released from Richmond. All week, every day, the deer paraded on the side of the road from the farm to the Centerville area where I live, as Michael's family passed through. All of us saw it. All commented about it. All felt it was God letting us know Michael was with us. All felt so honored as they passed through the parade of deer each day.

The funeral came and went like a haze or a fog. Then back to Tammy's to eat and each go to their separate places. I hid in the bedroom until most of the people left. I had no more strength to be around people. Later I went outside and sat at the picnic table Michael and I had sat at many times, the place where he shared his goals and dreams with me. I imagined he was just over at his house, which I could see from where I sat. I saw people going and coming from his house. I didn't understand why there wasn't any yellow ribbon around his house. Why the police allowed just anyone to enter the crime scene.

Soon my brother James, who actually was a cousin but acted like a big brother, came out and sat with me. I told him he was sitting in the same seat Michael had sat when he asked me to buy that three acres and trailer next door to his mama. He had said he would be on his own, but close enough to eat his mama's good cooking. James just sat and cried with me as we both stared at Michael's house. We had such a closeness, we didn't have to share words, we could just be there together.

Later that afternoon, the immediate family and a few friends went back up to the grave. We wanted pictures of the flowers while they were still so beautiful. Many cameras were flashing but not much talk. You will be amazed how important every picture becomes when that is all you have left of a loved one.

Days passed and we were busy with Michael's business and the details of the investigation, the 4th of July had come and gone. I had even gone to the beach with my sister Joyce. She felt we needed to get Alexis and Grace away together for a while. Alexis was only five years old and loved Michael so much. She had already lost her own brother Joseph (JoJo) in her short years on earth, and didn't understand why God took Michael too. It was a good idea Joyce had to get us away to look at new stuff, she said. At the beach we focused on the girls, enjoying the beach and seeing new scenes. It did help us to heal a little. Every deer picture on a shirt and every young boy about nineteen reminded me of the pain in my heart for Michael. But I pushed the tears away and focused even harder on the girls having fun.

One day after we had returned from the beach, I woke up and the Holy Spirit told me to go and develop the funeral film. I figured God was ready for me to move on with life and get it done. But like any other day when I really don't want to deal with something, I came up with many excuses not to go to Wal-mart and get it done. But the Holy Spirit wouldn't stop bugging me to get the film developed. Finally around four p.m. I gave in and replied, "Okay Lord. I will go to Wal-mart and get the funeral pictures developed, even though I really don't care to look at them. I will go just so you will stop bugging me. But if you don't mind, I will do the beach film also." Being a smart butt! The funeral pictures were the last thing we wanted to look at. But I did it to please the Holy Spirit. Not in the right attitude, but hey he is Father/Mother God. Besides I missed my joy within and I really did want that back.

After they were developed, in the car I looked at the pictures. I fought back the tears as I asked the Holy Spirit what he wanted me to see. With each picture I looked at, I felt the anger stronger and stronger rise up within me. I had so much anger and unforgiving toward that so-called girlfriend. (I had a few other choice names I thought about, but refused to write them down) that I was battling with inside.

I had attended The Worship Center to help me forgive and get my joy back. I had also spoken with Rev. Ed from the Superet Light Church in Washington D.C. almost every day. I read the words of Jesus daily and listened to Bible tapes and prayed. The Lord knew I wanted to release it and feel joy again, but I just couldn't let it go yet. Every time I thought about Michael not in his physical body, I would get angry all over again at the person that caused it and the police department. I was about to put the pictures in my purse because my eyes had become so blurry, I could barely see them anyway, when I saw the picture.

"That's it," I shouted, "Isn't it? Lord that's it!" I wiped the tears from my eyes and looked real close. "That's it." I took out my reading glasses and looked even closer and shouted in my car, "That's it. That's it, Lord. I am so sorry for not obeying you earlier. Please forgive me. Thank you, thank you, Holy Spirit."

Michael was in that picture with Michelle and Jonathan at his own funeral, just as clear as anything. I jumped out of the car and ran back in Wal-mart. I knew the lady back there thought I had flipped out of my mind but was just too nice to say it. I said, "Look at this picture. It is Michael in the spirit. Make me five copies of that picture."

She looked at it and said, "Mrs. Phillips, that might be a light from the church."

I answered, "No, it's not. But to make sure, I will ride up there tonight and see if there is a light out there anywhere. Please make the copies."

As she turned and looked at my face she touched my shoulder and said, "Or maybe you are looking at your grandson's spirit. Some people believe in that stuff, you know." Tears filled my eyes and I just nodded in agreement with her as she proceeded to make my copies.

I knew no one would believe me. They had to see the picture for themselves and see what they see. I had lived with the gift of discernment for sixty years and met many people who didn't believe or were too afraid to believe.

While I waited on the copies of Michael's picture, the Holy Spirit reminded me of this one experience. I had walked up to this black lady at work one day, after seeing her in a vision, and said, "I just saw your baby boy born. He is black as tar and fat as a watermelon. But he will grow up tall and brown skinned and very handsome. He is a warrior for God. God has many warriors born in this generation. The good news is you don't have a very good husband right now, but the Lord says when he sees this baby born he will drop to his knees and repent. He will give his heart to God and serve him all the days of his life."

Well, the look on her face told me I had better get back to my station as fast as I could move. When I got back to my table, Patricia asked, what did you say to that woman? When I told her, she laughed so hard she peed in her pants.

Needless to say I stayed away from that woman until she came in one day and announced she was pregnant. Then I walked over and asked her what she thought that night when I told her. She said she thought I was crazy. But when she went home and told her mama, her mama said, "You better pay attention to that white woman, girl."

Then the lady said she was afraid of me until she got pregnant. How did you do that? She asked. Did you know I wanted a baby but couldn't have one?

I replied, "Well, your womb won't close now. So after this baby, you might want to take birth control for awhile until you want a baby girl. And I don't know anything unless the Holy Spirit shows me." I was blunt! Just plain old blunt in my younger years.

Years later at the Halifax ball field, I saw this young boy, tall, with the most beautiful brown skin out on the ball field with Michael. I asked Tammy what his name was, but she didn't know. About that time this couple with a baby girl walked up smiling all over themselves. She looked straight at me and said, "Did you see your boy on that field?"

My whole body lit up as I smiled all over myself and replied, I knew it was him. I just asked Tammy who that boy was talking to Michael. But she didn't know his name and added he was playing on Michael's team. He was so drawn to Michael. When I looked out over that field, they both were shining like bright stars. I just knew that boy was one spoken by God on this earth. Look at them. They act like they have known each other all their life, not just met.

Well, of course she shared the rest of the story and how it all came to pass just like the Holy Spirit had said. And she added we got in a church after he was born that teaches us about such things, and I want to thank you. You made a believer out of us just by obeying the Holy Spirit.

About that time the lady was shaking my arm and saying my copies were finished. Would I like to pay there or up front? I landed back into reality again and replied right here.

That picture might not be something the police department would use in the investigation, but I knew it had a purpose. Why else would God show it to me? Would anyone else even see it? Like so much more evidence the sheriff's department refused to look at and wouldn't even investigate. I wasn't about to share this picture with anyone but family. God had been revealing clues every day from Michael's home and friends, encouraging us daily. Every time I began to cry, when I heard something else bad that girl had done or was doing, God made me remember that verse, where God said in his word, "Touch not my anointed, and do my prophets no harm."

The hardest job we had was turning it loose and let God investigate and expose. As far as I was concerned, this picture was one more piece of the evidence added to our collection. Proving God was investigating and exposing at his own time and in his own way, and is using his own people. I had to remind myself daily that Michael belonged to God before he was ever conceived in the womb, and he still belonged to God now.

We knew Michael was revealing the whole story of that last hour he was on this earth, June 21st 2008 at his home. As time passed, Michael showed us every detail of his passing and gave proof. Oh yes, rest assured, crimes may go unsolved on this earth, but every detail and word is recorded in heaven. Judgment day will come. Justice will be served.

And we know where Michael is. Michael is where Jesus is and where we shall be also. As long as we stay in Christ, we will see Michael. We will see Christ also, as well as all our other loved ones. A cloud of witnesses are all around us all the time. Our loved ones aren't silent or invisible to those who believe and live in the Christ light.

So if I had one message to leave with you, it is to say for you to walk in the truth, and Jesus Christ is that Truth. Christ and the Holy Spirit Mother God, I call him, and my Father God is three, yet One Creator God of all and in all. You might call him The Most High God or The Creator, but know one thing: we don't walk alone. We are surrounded by our God and our loved ones. Understanding will come!

Michael came to earth by the spoken word. He left us twenty years from the day the Archangel Gabriel announced his birth in a dream to me. The same archangel that announced to Abraham that he was having a son, in the old testament of the Bible, announced Michael's conception and birth. The same archangel that announced John the Baptist in the new testament of the Bible announced Michael's. The very same Archangel Gabriel that announced Jesus the son of the LIVING GOD to Mary announced Michael's birth. It has a meaning, and we will soon understand what that meaning is.

Over the years I can only share the children that have been announced by the Archangel Gabriel or the Holy Spirit through me, and there are many. But I know there are so many more children that have been born on this earth by the spoken word in my generation and my children's generation and grandchildren's generation. I have spent my last twenty years looking for those young children of light all over the world. When I hear them speak or listen to them on a tape or in music, I know them. God calls them "The Children of Light" or "The Children of God." What that means, I don't know yet. But one thing I feel very sure of, and that is children are gifts from God, and God doesn't like it when his gifts are rejected or abused.

Did Michael know he was going to heaven on June 21st 2008 on that horrible day for all of us that loved him? No! I don't think so, but he was ready to die any time. Michael grew up knowing about his conception. He knew he was sent to earth by God for a purpose. When he met this girlfriend, he couldn't believe the stories she told of her childhood. When he spoke of it to us, he cried like a baby. You could see it broke his heart to think one of God's little creatures had been treated the way she claimed she had been.

He would say, "Nanny, how can anyone treat a human being like that?" Michael made excuses for her outrage and angry fits (he called them). He would say she didn't know love. That she didn't know love was a person who lives inside of us. He would say, "Nanny, I have been loved all my life. Life is so good to me. My family has always been there for me. She has no one that loves her. She was raised around drugs and alcohol. She was put in a room with dogs and had to eat and sleep with dogs. That's what she tells us. Nanny, her childhood was horrible, according to her. She was taken away from her parents because they made her do things for drugs. Oh Nanny, she needs us to show her love. She doesn't understand love, Nanny."

How can we understand unless we suffer? Even God said he couldn't understand humans, and became a man and suffered so he could understand us. Jesus laid his life on a cross and cried out, "Father, forgive them, for they know not what they do."

I know and replay in my mind the love and words Michael has spoken. Someone said in one of their letters that Michael taught them how to love and be at peace. If you had the chance to know the real Michael, consider yourself blessed. If you had the chance and rejected him and still live in your body, you can still accept Jesus as God and savior and know him. For us who knew him and loved him and only wanted the best for him, we are forever thankful to God for him. To trust us just that little while with one of his precious gifts and give us the chance to know love in the flesh, we are honored. We are thankful to Jesus Christ. For it was Jesus who is the light, who is the Creator, who made it possible for us to live and never die.

I don't know how others believe. I only know what we have experienced from the spirit world and choose to believe. There surely is no such thing as death in Christ. As God said, "Don't fear him who can destroy the body. But fear him who can destroy the spirit, soul and body."

Saint Paul said, "Out of the body is present with the Lord."

We believe as soon as Michael left his body, he was present with the Lord. That is our belief, and we aren't trying to convince anyone else to believe that way. You be led by the Holy Spirit and believe according to the power within you.

We believe Michael is in the third heaven with Lil' Tommy, JoJo and all of our other loved ones, but most of all, he is in God. The peace that Michael and Christ left in Michael's home is there to this day.

Do I still cry? Yes! Some days more than others, and God always comforts me. Michael has revealed himself in many ways to many of his loved ones and friends, and continues to reveal himself to us. He continues to talk with us to this day.

From time to time on certain days, the five-mile parade of deer still honor us when we pass by. Hundreds of people have looked at that picture, and without us telling them anything have seen and testified they see Michael in that picture. The first Christmas after his passing, he spoke to his immediate family at different times but the same message.

"I am alive. I will never leave you. I am with you always. Look for me. Hear me when I speak." He speaks the same words we heard Jesus speak in the Bible. He and God are truly one, is our belief.

Matthew 3: 1-12 {KJ} "God is able of these stones to raise up children unto Abraham."

Isaiah 60: 1 "Arise! Shine! For your light (fire) is come,

and the Glory (fire) of the LORD is (risen) raised upon you."

Michelle and Michael
in front of his home
On
the farm he loved so much.

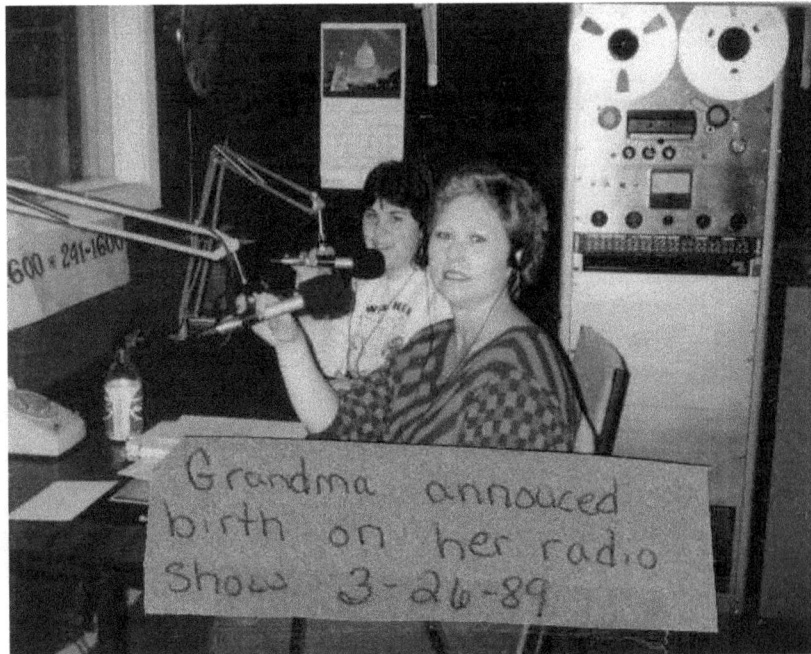

Nana Carolyn and Penny at her Radio Talk Show

Proud Nana Carolyn
and Michael at his 1st birthday party

Michael and His Deer Shirts!
2005

Christmas 2007
Nana had given the meaning of his name in Christ's words!

Michael and His Nana Carolyn

Michael, in the spirit, Michelle and Jonathan, on the day of Michael's funeral

I hope you can see how Michael was lying when he was shot and where the person was standing who shot him. If you look closer, you will see Michael's whole face as it appeared on his physical body, also a heavenly host of angels and/or loved ones.

CHAPTER FOURTEEN

WHY I BELIEVE MICHAEL WAS and IS AN ENDTIME SIGN

CHAPTER FOURTEEN

WHY I BELIEVE MICHAEL WAS and IS AN ENDTIME SIGN

I believe Michael was love in the flesh, based on the meaning from the Bible as I understand love, and based on Michael's words, "She doesn't know love, Nanny."

All of Michael's life he just loved people and respected them for who they were. Compared to Jesus, who was love in the flesh and who said, "Forgive them, for they know not what they do." Jesus loved his enemies with a true love. He forgave us not because we deserved it, but because he was love. He gave his life, the most precious gift anyone can give, and love gives.

We cannot do enough or be enough to save ourselves. Jesus said he who has the son has life already. All we have to do is trust Jesus.

With Michael, Jesus manifested himself, just like he did with my nephew, Lil' Tommy. We become what we worship, and worship is obedience to truth. We go into life and that is called resurrection power. All because of Jesus, I am so grateful to God the Father, God the Son, and God the Holy Spirit, for Michael.

Allow me to explain it to you this way. It was February 17th, 1980 when I saw and felt God's presence in my daddy's car. It was on a Monday the day after we had just buried his body. It was on that date that Jesus Christ appeared unto me and touched me on the right shoulder, and said "Why do you cry? Where he is, is where I am, and where you shall be also."

Then just one month later on April 17th,, 1980, my nephew, Lil' Tommy, we called him, was born. When I saw him, I saw his spirit. He was full of light and his eyes sparkled like the stars. I knew the change had taken place within me after Jesus appeared unto me in daddy's car.

When I asked God in prayer what it meant, He replied, "It was time to awaken, arise and shine." Later after I returned home from my brother's, I looked up those words and found them in the book of Isaiah 60.

One year later on April 17th, 1981, I had gone to bed and was awakened by Jesus Christ. He stood by my bed and said, "Arise, for the glory of God is come upon you." (Isaiah 60 again)

I immediately arose up from my body and stood beside him in all light, just like he was. I could sense he was wiser and more powerful, but as far as looks go, he was all light and so was I. Then he transmitted to me for me to look, and when I looked, I saw my own body lying dead on the bed. I bowed to worship him, to thank him, for allowing me to have life after physical death. But instead he touched my left shoulder and said, "Arise, my child, for it is not your time to leave."

I began to cry and begged him to let me stay with him in this glorious light. But instead he said, "You must go back. For your children need you." Then he waved his right arm and showed me my three little children, Tammy, Jay and Penny. Instantly I was back in my physical body.

When I awoke I was crying and pinching my right arm. Then I realized I was awake in my body and it had life again. I sat up real fast and began touching my body all over to see if it really was alive. Then I heard feet and looked and saw my children as they ran to my bed. They jumped up on the bed and into my lap and hugged me, crying, "Mama, Mama, are you alright? You were screaming, Jesus. Jesus please let me stay."

I grabbed the three of them and said, "Yes, Mama is just fine." Then I kissed them all on their foreheads and they crawled in under the covers with me. Soon they were fast asleep. I smoked a cigarette and even after I realized the time I decided to call my pastor anyway.

He answered the phone. "Rev. Grant here, how may I help you?"

I immediately apologized for waking him at 6:30 a.m. but I told him this couldn't wait. I had to tell someone or bust.

He said, "Alright, Carolyn, what is it that couldn't wait until 8 a.m.?"

So I began to share the spiritual experience and told him I wasn't sure if it was real or I was losing my mind. When I finished, I heard nothing but silence for a second and thought he had dropped off to sleep.

Then he said, "I don't know what it means exactly, but I have preached all of my life and prayed that God would give me such a revelation. I believe you have just had a dream about the afterlife. Carolyn, listen to Jesus's words and listen very carefully, for I have a feeling he is about to move you up higher into God. I believe it is a sign for this generation. I believe it is time we understand all Jesus did for us and all the Holy Spirit is doing in us and through us. Your Aunt Ellen has told me about some of your spiritual experiences. I couldn't advise her about such matters no more than I can advise you this morning. But if you will allow me, I would love to come and sit in your presence as you tell me again just what you have experienced. I would like to take notes and study it out in my Bible. When I get an understanding, I will give to you what God shows me. Is that a deal?"

I agreed and we did meet that day.

Several months later, Rev. Grant called and asked if he could come by and visit with me. When he stopped by, he said, "God was revealing to my generation the resurrection life. That the old was finished and the new had awakened." He said just as surely as he believed Saul saw the resurrected Christ and was changed to Saint Paul, he believed I had seen the resurrected Christ and my name and life style would also change.

Then he closed his Bible and hugged me ever so tightly. When he pulled back from me, that's when I saw his tears. He looked into my eyes and said, "I will keep you in my prayers as long as God gives me breath, and I will remember you always."

It was several years later when my husband decided he didn't want our marriage or children and left us. Several years after that when I met Sam and we married and moved to Jacksonville, Florida. That is where I met Uncle Early and Aunt Sylvia and began sitting under their teachings concerning revelation

I remembered what Rev. Grant had told me and shared it with Uncle Early. That's when Uncle Early said that Israel became a nation in 1948, and it was the time of the awakening. He said all babies that were born from 1948 until the next visitation would experience God in power and glory, and not have to suffer as his and his grandparents had suffered. The very fact that I saw God's presence in my daddy's car on February 17th, 1980 and Lil' Tommy was born April 17th, 1980 during Passover, which the children of light were being born upon this earth. He said in time the Berlin wall would fall, but not by men's hands, and in that year, children of light would arise. He continued to share with me that some children of light would die at an early age because just their birth would put Satan on the rampage. That the time was soon approaching when children would pass like flies.

Little did I know that day in 1982 that I would be the one that would receive the three dreams in 1988, the same year that the Berlin wall fell and not by men's hands, and God would send his own personal angel to announce the birth of Michael, my grandson. It was only eight years from 1980, just as Uncle Early had said. He said the numbers seven, eight, ten and twelve carried much end time revelation.

Little did I know that day in 1982 that what Uncle Early had shared, what God had showed him, that in just ten short years from the announcement of Michael's birth, my nephew Lil' Tommy would have cancer and pass as I watched him rise from his physical body on March 14th, 1998.

On the Wednesday before Lil Tommy passed, God sent me to the Lubbock Hospital around 4 a.m. to announce, "This is resurrection day." I didn't have a clue what it meant, but it was the same day that the doctors told us if Lil' Tommy was getting a miracle, he had better get it in a few days.

Then on Saturday morning, March 14th, 1998, God spoke again in a strong voice, "This is total restoration day." Still I had no clue as to what it meant. But at 12:20 p.m. I witnessed Lil' Tommy in all light arise up out of his body and fly to his mama and daddy. I watched as the nurses ran to call Tommy and Carol. I sat and waited in Lil' Tommy's room as the other nurses cleaned his body up before they arrived and felt the stillness. Then when they arrived and entered his room I felt total peace, a heavenly peace enter with them.

Then I saw Lil' Tommy with them, and he never left their side that day. We all witnessed Lil' Tommy flying beside the car as we traveled to Clovis N.M. from the hospital. We all experienced such heavenly events that day that it would fill its own book. It was the saddest day I had ever experienced, yet the most glorious day any human could experience. For forty days Lil' Tommy stayed with us, spoke with us, appeared unto us and taught us about spiritual things that just blew our minds.

The same happened when Michael left his body. I saw him and Christ standing over his body, and he stayed for forty days. He gave us what we needed to forgive and live in peace for the remainder of our days on earth.

Remember that love covenant, for it has given us that relationship with God. All conditions are fulfilled, and all we need to do is focus on the promises of life. The only way I know how to share my love for Michael is by sharing the story of another son. One who came and gave us love so we could love one another. We all are so loved by God. We are His love children, his very own family and he has such great plans for us all. All we have to do is believe and experience the heavenly glory that has already been accomplished for us. Heaven's atmosphere is love!

Michael and Lil' Tommy both, as well as many children all over the world, are all light, which means all love within. Whether they live or pass from their bodies, they are love. I John 3:1 says, "Behold what manner of love the Father has given unto us." I John 4: 16 says, "God is all love. Abide in love and love abides in you." Then in Romans 8: 32-39 it says, "We cannot be separated from love." And First Corinthians 13 says, "If we have not love, we have nothing."

Michael, as well as Lil' Tommy, fit every criteria of an Endtime sign based on their nature and character. For love creates and builds up. Love adds to what it has and shares it with others. All of God's goodness was lavished upon those who knew both of those boys.

Michael gave us more love and joy in nineteen years than most people give their whole seventy years or more. He left us with no bad memories or any regrets, as well as Lil' Tommy. Both were a blessing unto their family and friends from birth until physical death. How many parents can actually say it and know its truth?

The Bible says God knew we would hurt him before the foundation of the world, yet he created us anyway. I believe Michael knew in his heart of hearts, but was so vulnerable he wouldn't allow himself to believe any evil against anyone. Love makes you very vulnerable. The more you love someone, the more deeply you are hurt by them.

God made a plan of salvation for us before the seventh day of rest. He also promised to reveal unto us all things that pertain to truth before they happened, so we would know that it was God who had spoken unto us.

I believe Michael was an Endtime sign because the same angel announced his birth as announced Jesus Christ. From the moment he was born, his nature and character was love, peace and joy like Jesus.

It was ten years from Lil' Tommy's death, which was 1998, that we lost Michael in 2008. Numbers are an Endtime sign in themselves. Lil' Tommy was born in April 1980 and passed March 14th, 1998, while Michael was born March 24th, 1989, and passed June 21st, 2008. Can you see the comparison of numbers there? Also, Passover is usually in March or April, which is one of God's most sacred days or feast.

Michael came from love and manifested love while upon this earth, and he returned to love.

For those that speak evil and tell lies about Michael, all I can say is, line up their nature and character with the love book called Jesus's words. I bet you will find they are opposite of love in nature and character.

Some children are not born in a family of love and never know what real love is. Michael, like Lil, Tommy, knew they were love, and loved, and spread their love around to all who would receive it.

I believe Lil' Tommy's and Michael's birth and deaths were an Endtime sign, as well as many other children. I believe all those children were and are love children, and were and are shining stars. They certainly did light up my life.

I believe they, like so many others, have set the stage for the soon return of Christ upon this earth. I believe that is why there have been so many abortions. For in the days of Jesus, they killed babies in order to kill the morning star, Jesus himself. I believe there is so much darkness upon this earth right now that others will begin to arise and shine like the stars they are. The darker the night, the brighter the stars will shine.

Therefore I believe, based on my own spiritual experiences, that we are living right now in Isaiah 60, "Awake, Arise and Shine, for the Glory of God is come upon you."

I believe Jesus came to awaken us. The Holy Spirit came to help us arise, and Father God will shine in us and through us on this very earth. All three yet one.

Just as surely as there were three dreams that announced Michael's birth, and Isaiah spoke of three things for us to do, awake, arise and shine, and there have been three God natures upon the earth, The Father, Son and Holy Spirit. I believe we haven't seen or experienced the heavenly glories that God has prepared for his children, but we will now.

In this book I have shared our doubts and fears as well as some of our beliefs. Now allow me to close with the Holy Spirit.

Rev. Bobby Ray said to Tammy when she hung between life and death with her son, Michael, "O My God, this child is born full of the Holy Spirit. He will live and come forth, and so will you."

What did he mean by that statement according to the Bible that made his words so powerful? How did we know whether he spoke truth or just wanted ego glory? What evidence do we have that proved Michael was born full of the Holy Spirit? How do we know those of us who came into Michael's presence were in the presence of the Holy Spirit manifested?

We know by the word of God! The Bible explains it to us, by explaining the nature and character of the Holy Spirit himself, or herself for those who believe the Holy Spirit is our Mother God image.

Acknowledge the Holy Spirit and he will reveal himself and give us revelation. Love the Holy Spirit's presence and love going deep into the Holy Spirit. He is so humble, gentle and kind, so full of peace, joy and assurance. He loves spending time with us and loves our intimate relationships. All we have to be is available. Rest in his love and confess his truths. He is the mind of love.

When you know the nature and character of the Holy Spirit, then you will recognize and realize when you walk in the presence of the Holy Spirit manifestation in others as well as yourself.

A person full of the Holy Spirit will open up and allow you to drink from their river of life. You will feel the trust in that person, be encouraged by them and built up by them. You will leave their presence feeling more alive, more at peace, more in love with life, than you felt before you entered their presence. You will recognize the quietness, the stillness and the silence, and know it is holy.

When you meet someone envious or jealous of such a person, full of the Holy Spirit, who make statements like they hate such a person who is always doing good, and so loved, then you know that person has some serious soul healing that needs to take place. When you meet such a person who desires to hook a person full of the Holy Spirit, hook them with alcohol, or perverted sex, or slander such a person, you will know such a person really needs to investigate their own soul before it is too late.

When you know you are in the presence of the Holy Spirit, in any person, you need to honor and bless that Holy Spirit within them. As Aunt Sylvia and Uncle Early sang, "When I see God in you, well I'm alright."

We are living in the thousand fold blessing, which means more than physical prosperity. There are three zeros in one thousand, that means three nothings and one something. That one something is the Most High God, Creator of all, who is Oneness. When you realize you are three parts, yet one, and when your spirit of flesh is zero, your spirit of soul is zero, and your spirit of spirit is zero, then all that remains is One. May God bless you and me a thousand fold. Amen.

It is only while we are asleep in the darkness, that we run away from and want to hate, be jealous and envious of the children of the Holy Spirit. It is only while we sleep in the darkness, that we love drugs, alcohol, perverted sex, violence, anger, war and rage. It is only while we walk around asleep, that we commit adultery, lie, steal and abuse others and don't like work or supporting families, or we're lazy and just want to play, like little children, and not be accountable or responsible for ourselves or our family or community or country. What do they need? They need to wake up. Once they wake up, then they can arise up out of all darkness and have no excuses or justifications. Then they will shine and bring glory to God our Creator.

A real relationship with the Holy Spirit is the cure for the walking dead or sleepwalking folks. There's a seven fold spirit or dimension if you want the fullness of the Holy Spirit. But you will need the Holy Spirit to get to the first step.

In John 16:5, Jesus said, "Now I am going to Him who sent me. It is to your advantage that I go away. The ruler of this world of darkness is judged."

In Acts chapter one, Jesus said, "I am going away. I have shown you the Kingdom of God. Now be led by the Holy Spirit."

Isaiah chapter eleven teaches us the nature and character of the Holy Spirit, as well as shows us the different dimensions. He also shows us that our closest friend on earth is the gift from God our Father of glory, which is the Holy Spirit.

In the book of Genesis in the Bible, a certain tree when eaten brings death, and death is separation or sleep.

In the Kingdom of God it's all about relationships. It's not about knowledge or study, but about relationships. The closer you walk with God the Creator, the more you become like him.

Jesus came to awaken us. The Holy Spirit came to move us so we could arise, grow up or mature. Jesus said, "When you see me, you see my Father."

You follow yourself if you want to, but you might be worse off than following the devil. Consider for a moment, if you are asleep on earth, then when you leave your physical body you will be asleep in the afterlife.

How well do you know the Holy Spirit? Ask yourself. Jesus kept his physical body when he died, arose, and ascended. We can keep our bodies and be changed into light. When do we plan to leave the earth with our spirit, soul and body? Do you know the difference between your spirit and the Holy Spirit? Jesus in physical form was to show us the Father.

Do you know who the Holy Spirit is; the Spirit of God; The Spirit of Truth; The Spirit that reveals; the Comforter like a mother? Do you know we can talk spirit to Spirit, and that's deep? When you study the Holy Spirit and see who he is, you will be amazed, but you will know him when you meet him. Thank you, and I hope you will study the Holy Spirit.

I believe the next eight years, from March 2008 until March 2016, will be the greatest harvest in world history. I believe you will see the released empowerment of revelation, greater than anytime the world has ever seen. I believe the earthquakes will be stronger and souls will run to God. I believe what is Jesus is mine now. What the Father gave to him, he in turn has given to me to enjoy. For the next eight years, soak in the Holy Spirit. Be ready, be willing, be prepared and keep your lamps burning. Meditate in the Holy Spirit, the river of life, the living waters. From March 2008 until March 2016, I believe more will have dreams and visions. There will be more visitations from the other side, more people experiencing transportation and wholeness. I believe the Holy Spirit is quickening us for signs and wonders. I believe love will reveal more understanding and he will wash and purify more, seal more, free more. There will be more fellowship, and more each day to understand the resurrection and restoration. For I believe this is Resurrection and Restoration Day! I believe the Holy Spirit calls the Bridegroom and Bride to come together in joy as one new man, with such boldness that even the wicked cannot deny him.

Believers, we are the dwelling place for the Holy Spirit. We are receivers. We are magnets. We are radio antennas.

Allow me to leave you with this warning: every generation has called the work of the Holy Spirit evil and demonic. Don't stay in ignorance. Arise up out of ignorance and come into the glorious light of God's mind. You will see the supernatural from this viewpoint. The Holy Spirit discernment doesn't judge what it doesn't understand, but seeks the kingdom of God. Be careful of speaking forth your ignorance, for you really don't want to grieve the Holy Spirit.

Let this be our prayer…Let me honor, you Holy Spirit. Fill us afresh daily. Fill every part of our being now. Reveal to us the heart and mind of our Creator. Touch us daily. We acknowledge you, Holy Spirit. Arise and shine, O Glory. Arise and shine like the stars, ever so bright. Let me refresh you, Holy Spirit. Let me give you glory, Holy Spirit. Let me bless you. I want to bless you, O Holy Spirit! Amen.

A Note to My Readers:

I want to thank you first of all for purchasing and reading my book. I hope you will tell others about it and Michael's amazing conception and birth. I hope you felt the love in Michael's story and will pass that on, as well, to your loved ones. I hope you cherish your family daily and make time for them while you have them. I truly hope you have a closer walk with God and a more personal experience with our Creator after reading my book. I hope you have enjoyed the little bit of Michael's life that we have shared with you as much as we have enjoyed sharing it with you. I hope it leaves you with HOPE.

I also hope you feel led to share your spiritual experiences with us. Just a note to us on how or what you received out of this book would be great. You may write to: 1059 Avondale Drive, Halifax, VA, 24558. If you would like your spiritual experience to be included in one of my future books, please let me know that as well. I cannot promise that it will be included, but it might be.

If you are a family that has been blessed to give birth to a child of light and you would like to share your experience with me, please write me at the above address.

If you are one who thinks I am crazy, then I pray that you will wake up before you depart this life.

I hope you will look for additional books of mine.

If God keeps me in good health, my next book about Michael will go into the details of his death, and the investigation, as to what was done, and what wasn't done. We will put the facts out there and let you, our readers, decide if Michael took his own life or if he was murdered by a jealous and outraged girl.

You read the opinions and facts of the case in *Michael, Suicide or Murder*. Then you decide. If you have any facts or have heard anything about Michael's case and want to share what you have seen or heard, then write us. For now, we say thank you!

Michael, we love you! To have known you was to know real love in this flesh life. Michael was love, living, breathing love!

We ask God to bless your short life on earth and use it for his glory. We ask that he bless your memory and good name. We ask God to bless all of you that knew him and all that had a personal experience and relationship with him.

We ask God to bless himself in your life, Michael. And our greatest hope is that God will get all of the glory. Now let God be glorified forever more!

We also ask God to reveal all the truth concerning your physical death and reveal all who are guilty, and may they come to justice. We ask God to help us understand and live in greater love and appreciation for family and friends, but most of all for you, O God, for all you do for each of us every day. We thank you for appreciation and for hearing us always.

I hope you have enjoyed the few pictures we have shared of Michael. And until we meet again, be blessed!

Back row: Austin, Michael, Michelle. Middle row: Alexis, Jayson, Jayden, Kalee.
Wyatt,
Nana Carolyn's Grandchildren
Thanksgiving 2007

WE LOVE YOU, MICHAEL!